Inspiring Ideas to Support Early Maths and Literacy

Inspiring Ideas to Support Early Maths and Literacy takes a play-based approach and draws on popular stories and rhymes to cover the key areas of mathematics and literacy. Full of practical, tried-and-tested ideas for developing understanding in mathematics and literacy, this book aims to help practitioners make these areas of learning exciting and meaningful for young children.

Each chapter shows how learning can be reinforced and brought to life through resources made from everyday materials, providing children with an enjoyable and positive learning experience. Key features include:

- clear instructions and full-colour photographs on how to make practical resources for indoor and outdoor environments
- vocabulary lists for inspiration and ideas for developing a new play space or overhauling an existing space
- key questions to consider when planning and designing an indoor or outdoor play space
- links to the Early Years Foundation Stage that will guide the development of a future playground and challenge providers to enhance their practice.

This practical resource will be essential reading for primary teachers, early years practitioners, students and all those interested in developing young children's confidence in mathematics and literacy.

Janet Rees is an independent education consultant who has a wealth of experience throughout the UK and abroad working with children, parents and teachers. Her particular interest is in the early years, and she has written many books and articles to support the learning of young children.

Inspiring Ideas to Support Early Maths and Literacy

Stories, rhymes and everyday materials

Janet Rees

Routledge
Taylor & Francis Group

LONDON AND NEW YORK

First published 2016
by Routledge
2 Park Square, Milton Park, Abingdon, Oxon OX14 4RN

and by Routledge
711 Third Avenue, New York, NY 10017

Routledge is an imprint of the Taylor & Francis Group, an informa business

British Library Cataloguing in Publication Data
A catalogue record for this book is available from the British Library

Library of Congress Cataloging in Publication Data
Names: Rees, Janet.
Title: Inspiring ideas to support early maths and literacy : stories, rhymes, and everyday materials / Janet Rees.
Description: Abingdon, Oxon ; New York, NY : Routledge, 2016.
Identifiers: LCCN 2015032878| ISBN 978-1-1388-2447-8 | ISBN 978-1-1388-2448-5 |
    ISBN 978-1-3156-4077-8
Subjects: LCSH: Games in mathematics education. | Mathematics—Study and teaching—Activity programs.
Classification: LCC QA20.G35 R44 2016 | DDC 372.7—dc23
LC record available at http://lccn.loc.gov/2015032878

ISBN: 978-1-138-82447-8 (hbk)
ISBN: 978-1-138-82448-5 (pbk)
ISBN: 978-1-315-64077-8 (ebk)

Typeset in Bembo
by Swales & Willis Ltd, Exeter, Devon, UK
Printed and bound in Great Britain by Ashford Colour Press Ltd, Gosport, Hampshire

Contents

Introduction   1

1. Paperware   2

2. Bags, boxes and cardboard tubes   13

3. Hair-related items   34

4. Number lines   46

5. Don't throw this away   65

6. Useful resources   76

Index   89

Introduction

The learning journey

Learning is a continuous journey and children take personal paths based on their own individual interests, experiences and the curriculum on offer. Throughout the journey, children build on what they have already experienced or learnt. Their needs and interests are central to the learning process.

The activities in this book have been designed to be very 'hands on' and will provide starting points to encourage and promote children's mathematical, scientific, creative, linguistic and personal and social areas of learning. The activities use cheap, often free or recycled, resources to inspire both you and your children no matter where the learning journey is taking place. This could be at home, in school, on the beach, in the park, in fact anywhere, anytime. The activities have been tried and tested with young children as well as older children working at the relevant level. They have been developed from the creativity of children themselves and then built upon to improve children's confidence, self-esteem, motivation and achievement. They encourage the development of the skills children need for adult life as well as the wider goal of developing the talents of the individual.

Child–centred learning is an approach to education that places the children and their needs at the centre. The focus is not on what is taught but on how effective learning should be promoted. This ensures that learning is an active, dynamic process in which connections between different facts, ideas and processes are constantly being made and developed. A creative environment allows all children to learn and discover as they set their own challenges and use all their senses. They will have opportunities to use flexible play materials and to use play materials flexibly.

> To live a creative life we must lose our fear of being wrong.
>
> Joseph Chilton Pearce, American author

I hope you feel inspired to find your own resources. Please share further ideas with me so that I can share them more widely.

I would like to thank Phillip Rees for taking the photographs used in the book.

Happy hunting!

Janet

P.S.

> We do not stop playing because we grow old; we grow old because we stop playing.
>
> George Bernard Shaw

Chapter 1: Paperware

This chapter looks at how paperware can be used to help children's communication and language, maths and vocabulary. It includes activities using paper plates, wrapping paper, serviettes, kitchen rolls and tablecloths.

Paper plates

Paper plates are one of the most useful mathematical models ever produced, and can be used in games to help children understand how 'more' and 'less' work. The main learning objectives for the following activities are:

Communication and language

Understanding: Children follow instructions involving several ideas or actions. They answer 'how' and 'why' questions about their experiences.

Vocabulary

Number, zero, one, two, three . . .

How many?

More, less, one more, one less

How did you work it out?

Start with

The same as

More than

Less than

To make this useful mathematical model, take two different-coloured, plain paper plates. Place one on top of the other and cut the radius (from the edge to the centre).

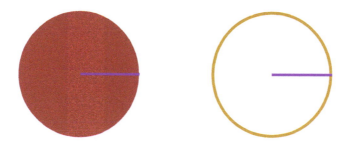

Separate them and slot one into the other.
Press them flat so that the top one turns on top of the lower one.
Children can cut their own if they are able.
Each child has a set.
At this point give time for the children to play with the plates, finding out how they move around and then move back again. Don't be too quick to ask questions. As with any new resource, children will work better if they are familiar with what they can do.
Now ask a question such as 'Can you show me more red than white?'
As long as more red than white is shown, whatever the child does will be correct. This allows much more opportunity to 'get the right answer'.
Continue with other instructions such as:
'Show me less red than white.'
'Show me the same amount of red and white.'
Ask the children to work in pairs and ask each other questions.
So we have looked at more than, less than and the same as.
Change one of the plates so that there are pictures showing.
Using the plates as before:
'Show me one flower.'
'Show me more than one flower.'
'Show me three flowers. Take one away. How many are left?'

This is where the play opportunity from before becomes useful. Children will know that to show more the plate is turned one way, and to show less it needs to be turned the opposite way.

By changing one of the plates there will be opportunities to go to higher numbers. Using pictures of animals can develop a link with 'Old MacDonald Had a Farm'.

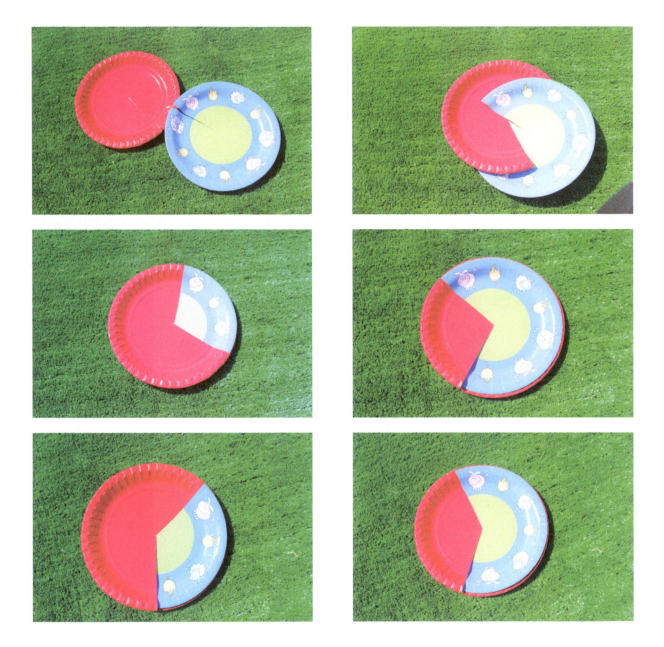

'Show me two chickens.'
'Show me four animals.'
'How many can you see?'

If there isn't a ready-made plate with pictures that interest the child, use pictures cut from wrapping paper, serviettes or downloaded from the internet, and stick them on.

Stick the pictures where you want them onto a plain white plate and cover the whole plate with a thin layer of PVA glue. This will help to keep the pictures in place when the plates are turned, and also gives a shiny finish so that the plates turn more easily. You can have one, two, three or more pictures according to the age, ability and interest of the child. And, of course, the size of the plate.

You can buy or recycle paper plates. For example, when planning a party for a child, choose paper plates that you can use afterwards. As long as there has been no jelly on the plate, they usually clean nicely with a damp cloth. Jelly makes them too soggy!

Wrapping paper

Wrapping paper is a cheap resource. Some of it is designed to appeal to children, being full of popular and contemporary characters suitable for a wide range of games. Why spend time drawing and colouring when it has already been done for you? (Unless you love colouring in! A legacy from your school days perhaps?)

Below are the main learning objectives for the following activities.

Communication and language

Understanding: Children follow instructions involving several ideas or actions. They answer 'how' and 'why' questions about their experiences.

Children have opportunities to experience a rich language environment and to develop their confidence and skills in expressing themselves.

Vocabulary

Number, zero, one, two, three …

How many?

Count

Game, match, same, different

Long, short, wide, narrow, thick, thin, longer than, shorter than

Curved, straight, across, up, down

Mathematics

Numbers: Children count reliably with numbers one to twenty.

They develop and improve their skills in counting, understanding and using numbers.

Children investigate and experience things and 'have a go'.

Active learning: Children concentrate and keep on trying if they encounter difficulties and enjoy achievements.

Creating and thinking critically: Children have and develop their own ideas, make links between ideas and develop strategies for doing things.

Look in any shop that sells wrapping paper and you will see what children are interested in. A great deal of research has been done to produce designs that children respond positively to. Use that research and buy a sheet of wrapping paper! Once an image has gone from duvet covers, curtains and wrapping paper, it generally means that children have moved on in their interests.

Use the pictures to make a variety of games such as:

Dominoes

A traditional set has 28 dominoes, but make the number lower for younger children. The aim is to make the game fun to play, but if the game takes too long, some children may give up before the end.

Glue the pictures onto the back of cereal packets. Invite the children to help spread the glue and possibly cut the pictures. Involve children as much as possible with the construction of games. They will be much more willing to play (although you may have to wait several days for the glue to dry!).

One of the wonderful things about dominoes is that anyone can learn the basics of picture-matching. Some children may need extra help so make the pictures large and colourful, without fussy backgrounds. Use textures such as sandpaper for house bricks ('Three Little Pigs') or fur fabric for animals. Add anything to help children distinguish between the pictures as long as the additions are well stuck on, in case children are tempted to pull them off and taste them!

The basis of most domino games is to lay down one domino next to another, so that the pictures, shapes, colours or spots match each other.

Don't always play in a straight line. Go wild and turn a corner sometimes.

Snap

Snap is a card game where all of the cards are shuffled and dealt equally to the players. The cards are left face down in a pile in front of each player.

Players take it in turn to take the top card from their pile and place it face up in the middle. When someone turns over a card that matches the card in the middle, the players race to be the first to say 'Snap!' That player then takes all of the cards from the centre pile.

The player who wins all of the cards wins the game.

As before, use tactile materials to highlight textures and use large, bold pictures. There is no good reason why children with physical or sensory disabilities should always work on any sort of separate programme. For most of them it is simply a question of access, and materials should be adapted to meet their particular needs so that they can work alongside their peers.

The pictures can be from any source. I usually look for wrapping paper first as that tends to be the cheapest. But they can be from an old book, greeting cards or children's own drawings. (I know these are cheaper than wrapping paper, but sometimes the drawings can be open to different interpretations!)

Another source of pictures is rubber stamps. A possible drawback to these is that they are often quite small.

Bingo

There is a huge amount of satisfaction that comes from shouting out the word 'BINGO!'

Bingo is an easy game to play. Once children understand the game, you can mix up the rules to make the game more interesting. It can be played as one-to-one or with a small group.

A bingo board consists of a 5 × 5 grid, but can easily be reduced to 3 × 3 or even 2 × 2.

Make your board by covering individual squares of the grid with pictures of your choice. The aim of the game is to cover all the squares on the grid with matching pictures.

The caller uses a matching set of cards or a spinner to match the pictures on the board. As the caller holds up a card or spins the spinner, the players must identify the picture on their boards and cover it.

When one player's board is covered, the game ends. If animal pictures are used, the children can make an animal sound instead of shouting 'BINGO!', or they can make a silly face or jump up and down. Asking the children to come up with their own ways is a good way of encouraging creativity.

Snakes and Ladders

Snakes and Ladders is a game that has interested generations of children and often their parents too! It is easy to play and a lot of fun. Make your own Snakes and Ladders board using the pictures on wrapping paper. Much easier than drawing all of those pictures. And use dough and card for the snakes and ladders.

Whenever possible encourage the children to help you design and make the board. You can use squares, circles, triangles or any other shape you want. They do not have to fit together with no spaces. Stick them on some coloured card or paper and let the colour show through.

As long as there is a start and a finish, the game can be as long or as short (in time) as you want it to be. You do not need to include numbers but you will need to draw arrows at the end of each row to show which way to go next.

Make the dough and roll snake shapes.

There are many different recipes for dough. In Chapter 6 there are three that I have found to be successful when working with young children.

Make some long, short, thin, narrow, fat, straight or curved snakes. Bake them slowly in the oven and then paint them.

Here is a very busy boy painting his own snakes.

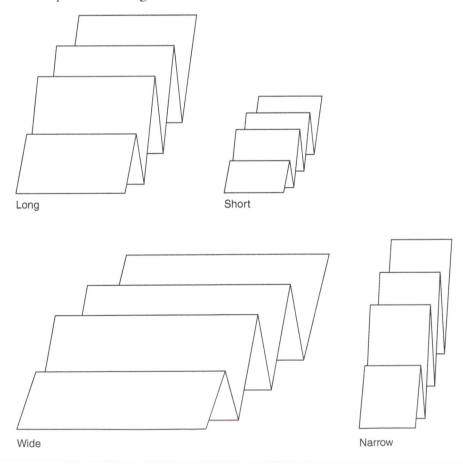

Fold card as a zigzag to make the ladders. Make them long, short, wide or narrow. Talk about what you and the children are doing so that they see the physical representation of the words you are using.

Long

Short

Wide

Narrow

Once the props have been made you need to get together the rest of the pieces. That's easy! Make your own dice and choose your own playing pieces. That's easy too. There are lots of ideas again in the resources section.

Put the snakes and ladders on the board and let the game begin.

Players take turns to throw the die and move that number of spaces along the board. The die could have spots, numbers or arrows showing which way to move.

Every time you play, the game will be different. More ladders and fewer snakes? Fine. More snakes and not so many ladders? Fine. Only grown-ups can use the snakes? That's fine too. As the children become more familiar with the game, change one rule at a time. Make the ladders different colours; a green one means have another go, a red one means miss a turn. Agree the new rules with the children *before* each game starts.

There are examples of other designs in the resources section. Use these as a starting point for you and the children. Change or adapt them as you want to. Link them with real-life experiences or with a favourite story or rhyme. The choice is yours.

Now here's a plan. Encourage your children to design and make their own game board. If it's their game, it has to be good. Give them chances to play the game. They may want to change it over time, or they may be happy with what they have done.

All the ideas that you have for your wrapping paper can be transferred to:

Serviettes

Simple bold designs are better for younger children so that they can focus on the main idea. Some designs have an animal taking up the whole serviette. This could be a cat, a caterpillar or even a chicken. These can be used as a simple number line. (There's more about number lines in Chapter 4: Number lines.) If the animal is also walking from left to right, that would guide the children into counting on.

Don't be tempted to write the numbers at the early stages, just count and play with the pictures. Make an animal trail that goes under, over and through obstacles or furniture.

When working and playing with serviettes, peel the back layer off before you stick the picture part onto card. If you leave the bottom layer on, the top layer (with the picture on) will gradually separate and fall off. If you can laminate the picture part, that will be better.

Some pictures can be used for simple counting such as the row of beach huts shown overleaf.

Link the picture with a story, such as *Beach* by Elisha Cooper, *Arthur's Dream Boat* by Polly Dunbar or *Teddy at the Seaside* by Amanda Davidson, or to real-life experiences of the children. Make the serviette into a game and you're ready to play. Use pebbles or shells as playing pieces to keep to the theme of the game board.

This serviette can be a game for two players, each having half of the whole picture. Use a simple die with a green arrow or a red arrow on each face. The players take turns to throw the die and move forwards or backwards according to the colour of the arrow: green to move forwards to the next hut and red to move to the previous one. The first player to reach the hut with the blue striped flag wins the game.

Some serviettes are made so that they can be cut into four equal-sized pieces. Then what?

- Cut several and use as snap cards.
- Cut several and use as pairs where the cards are placed face down on the table and each player chooses two cards. If they match, that player takes them. If they don't,

the cards are placed face down again and the next player has a turn. The player with the most cards when they have all been taken is the winner. HINT: Don't put too many cards down at the start. This makes it much too difficult for young children. Gradually increase the number as they become more confident.

- Cut two sets, one for the child and one for the adult. The adult sets out all four pictures on the table so that the child can see. The child closes his eyes and one of the pictures is removed. When the child opens their eyes they take the missing picture from their own set to replace the one that has been taken. Check with the removed card that they are the same. Repeat. When the child is confident, adult and child swap their roles.
- Use a whole serviette as a bingo base board. Cut another one into four pieces and play a game of bingo. This involves simple picture-matching.

Kitchen rolls

Oh my goodness, what can I say about kitchen rolls? If you see a pattern or design you like, buy it immediately as they change so quickly.

I have collected many different ones over the years. Some I still use, some I keep in the garage waiting for a comeback! But I am always looking for more. Particular times of the year or events are always good for a spending spree: Easter, Christmas, Red Nose Day, Sport Relief, for example. Kitchen rolls are readily available in all supermarkets and I have, on occasion, brought them back from countries that I have visited all over the world.

Using the pictures: Cut them, sort them, hide them, sequence them, laminate them, share them, compare them, use them to make a story. And as a bonus, once you have peeled the back off the kitchen roll, leaving just the picture you want, you will still have that spare paper to mop spills and/or children!

Tablecloths

Although paper tablecloths are available, they don't tend to have staying power as children scribble and scramble over them, so I have taken the liberty of adding plastic to this paper section!

These cloths are ideal for pairs or small groups of children to play a game on a larger scale. They can have a designated area marked by a permanent marker. In this way several pairs or groups can play at the same time – a perfect way to develop social skills and communication.

Handy hints

- Grade and classify the games in order to achieve a balance between different levels of ability. Start with games of chance so that players have an equal chance of success.
- Check that the children have the prerequisite skills needed to have at least a chance of success.
- Work with one group at a time when introducing a new skill or a new game. This group can then tell others how to play.
- Introduce new games at regular intervals.
- Involve the children in making decisions when creating a new game.
- Make new games using inexpensive materials so that the children don't have to worry too much about either the board or the pieces.
- Remember that a game is only worth playing if it is right for the children who are playing it.
- Minimise any written instructions and explanations. Remember that mathematics has a very strong visual element and capitalise on this whenever you can to show meaning. Make frequent use of games where the rules are picked up quickly by watching a demonstration.
- Peer group talk is important in helping children to make sense of and apply mathematical ideas. It helps if English language beginners can talk with other children or adults who speak the same home language when they are doing practical group activities or playing mathematical games.

Involve parents and carers

Out-of-class activities need to be frequent, short and focussed. They should be varied, interesting and fun, so that they motivate children, stimulate their learning and foster different learning skills.

Playing games will help the child gain confidence and develop a clearer understanding of basic number skills. Each game can be adapted and children should be encouraged to then make up games of their own. Be sure to negotiate suitable rules before play begins – this stops arguments.

Make games for a games library within your setting, so that children can take games home. They can play with parents, guardians, siblings, grandparents, aunts, uncles or even the couple next door!

Be creative! Remember, don't always make games *for* the children, make them *with* the children.

Have fun.

Chapter 2: Bags, boxes and cardboard tubes

This chapter looks at how bags, boxes and cardboard tubes can be used to help children's communication and language, maths and vocabulary creativity. Below are the main learning objectives for the following activities.

Communication and language

Listening and attention: Children listen attentively to stories.

Understanding: Children follow instructions involving several ideas or actions. They answer 'how' and 'why' questions about their experiences.

Speaking: Children develop their own narratives and explanations by connecting idea or events.

Reading: Children read and understand simple words.

Vocabulary

Heavy, light, heavier than, lighter than, heaviest, lightest

Full, empty

Compare

Count, count on, count back

Zero, one, two, three . . .

First, last

None, how many?

Mathematics

Shape, space and measures: Children use everyday language to talk about weight, size, capacity, position and distance to compare quantities and objects, and to solve problems.

Paper bags have been an American staple since they were invented there in the late 1800s, and are now widely used throughout the world. In addition to carrying groceries and packing lunches, there are many useful things you can do with a paper bag. Its strong and sturdy construction makes a paper bag perfect for present-wrapping; as a dressing-up vest with holes cut in the base and sides for the arms and head to go through; a storage bag; writing paper; a book cover. Ideas are included here to show how bags can also be used more creatively with children to cover the objectives stated.

What is a box? There are plenty of opportunities to discuss this with children and allow them to give their own ideas. Be aware that their ideas may not be the same as yours! Boxes come in many shapes and sizes, holding a variety of objects. There are also, of course, homemade ones, which can come in a wealth of different shapes and sizes. The activities in this chapter allow children to develop imagination, creativity and mathematical ideas and language.

Cardboard tubes can be found in many guises: long, short, wide, narrow, for domestic and industrial use. Have you ever seen a child crawl through the tube that had carpet rolled around it? Look in your kitchen for smaller versions such as those holding foil, cling film or paper products. The ideas in this chapter build on what children know and understand about a tube but then build on this to allow them to develop their own ideas.

Paper bags

Let's begin with paper bags, which also make splendid puppets!

Puppets

Challenge the children to 'Make a puppet that looks just like you'.

This can be a wonderful pair/share activity or an individual activity where mirrors are available for the children so that they can see their reflection.

For pair/share sit two children opposite each other. One is the maker of the puppet, the other is the teller. The puppet-maker has the paper bag, colouring materials, scissors, and paper (for hair). The teller looks at the puppet-maker's face and tells their partner exactly what they see. A non-threatening way of communicating information to your friend! When one puppet is made, the children swap roles.

When making a paper bag puppet, the first thing to do is to find a suitable size bag.

Lay the paper bag flat with the opening facing towards you and the flap at the bottom showing. Use paint, crayons or pencils to draw facial features on the flap. For eyes, glue on two googly eyes or buttons (or you can draw them on the bag). You can also draw clothing below the flap or glue fabric scraps or coloured paper on.

Lift the flap up carefully and draw or stick on a tongue.

Close the face and draw an upper lip under the nose and a lower lip just below the flap. Add hair by cutting some lengths of wool or paper. Sometimes the scissors used in school make cutting fabric or wool difficult. It is better for the children to cut what they need rather than an adult cutting what they think the children need. Glue the 'hair' on to the top edge or the front of the flap, near the top. To use the puppet, put your hand into the bag and place your fingers in the flap. Move your fingers up and down to make it 'talk'.

There are lots of variations on this theme. Children can make puppets that will then be part of a puppet show, or they can use them to act out a scene for the role-play area. Or use them for familiar rhymes and stories. The characters from traditional tales such as Cinderella or Sleeping Beauty or a favourite story of the child can all be made. Encourage the children to work together in pairs or small groups to 'write' and act a play for the rest of the group. 'Write' can mean a child's own early writing or beginning to use their knowledge of phonics where they will be linking sounds and letters.

Communication and language development involves giving children opportunities to experience a rich language environment; to develop their confidence and skills in expressing themselves; and to speak and listen in a range of situations. Using puppets is one way of allowing children to express themselves effectively, beginning to show awareness of their listeners' needs. They can develop their own narratives by connecting ideas or events.

The Gingerbread Man or *The Gruffalo* would be good stories for sequencing a story. Different children can take the parts of the characters and tell the story through their puppets.

Make a zoo. Make a farm. Make an alien landscape.

Ask children for their own ideas. Encourage parents and carers to make their own puppets too.

Have a puppet day! Make a hat from a paper bag to wear for the day. You can wear it on your head or you can wear it over your head! Decorate with as much creativity as time and money allow. *But* remember to make sure there is no wet glue inside your hat, or you may end up wearing it for longer than you wanted to!

Stories

Some stories just cry out for the use of bags to engage, delight and challenge children.

'The Three Little Pigs' is one that I use a lot. You will need three pink bags. I usually use sparkly bags as they have a bit more appeal for younger children. You will also need some straw, some sticks and a house brick, all of which need to fit into the bags.

Or find some pig bags.

At this point I ought to mention that a house brick in a bag that has handles may not be a good idea for some children. If this is the case, for whatever reason, substitute something that looks like a house brick, such as a wooden block or a cardboard box. Cover it with PVA glue and then roll it in sand. This will give it a texture similar to a brick. However, when the items are put into their bags, the bag of straw must be the lightest, the bag of sticks heavier than the straw but lighter than the brick, and the 'brick' bag needs to be the heaviest of all.

Ask the children which bag *they* think is the heaviest. Many young children will think it is the bag of straw as this bag is packed so full that no more straw will fit in. Whichever bag they choose, ask them to compare it with the weight of a different bag. Please don't tell them that they are wrong. If you ask the children 'What do you think?' they cannot be wrong if it's what they think. They are giving you an opinion. Give them opportunities that will allow them to change their mind. If you have balance or bucket scales this would be a good time to use them. If not, the children can become the scales themselves. Whichever hand is holding the heavier bag should be lower than the other hand.

Ask other children to come and give their opinions on the choices made.

Put the lightest bag back on the table and let the children use the other two bags to put them in order of weight. This may take some time! Some changes may need to take place to get them in the final order. Put the lightest on the left, the heaviest on the right and the other one in the middle.

This way of arranging the bags follows the rule of the number line, but here the more you move to the right the more weight there is, as opposed to a number line where quantity is represented by a number. There is more about number lines in Chapter 4.

Make labels that can be put against the bags, but make sure that the children understand that these labels can be moved if necessary.

Cut sets of pig shapes facing opposite ways. Ask the children to place one set in front of the bags to show the pigs walking from the lightest to the heaviest. And then the other set walking from the heaviest to the lightest.

Change the bags you use and a whole new world opens up!

These bags work for the rhyme 'Five Little Speckled Frogs'. This time use the bags for quantity rather than weight. Use numbers to put the bags in sequence.

You will need fifteen individual bugs. Any sort, any colour. For some children I like to use different colours to represent numbers. I have found that it helps the young or less confident child. Once children are confident in matching quantity to the relevant number the colours can go. The next step is to use a variety of bugs so that children are looking at quantity and recognising that 3 is 3 whatever the bugs are.

Begin the activity!

Class chant the rhyme of 'Five Little Speckled Frogs'.

Five little speckled frogs
Sitting on a speckled log
Eating their nice delicious grubs, yum yum.
One jumped into the pool
Where it was nice and cool
And that left just four speckled frogs glug glug.

Continue until there are no frogs left.

Place all the frogs on the floor or table so that the children can see them. Children take turns to throw a die marked 1, 2, 3, 1, 2, 3 and take the corresponding number of bugs. The numbering on the die can suit the children who are playing. You may want to incude zero or you may not. You may want to work with just one and two or go the whole range to six. The choice is yours.

Instead of numbers you can use the pictures of the bugs but make them black and white so that the players don't get confused with the colours. They need to match quantity not colour.

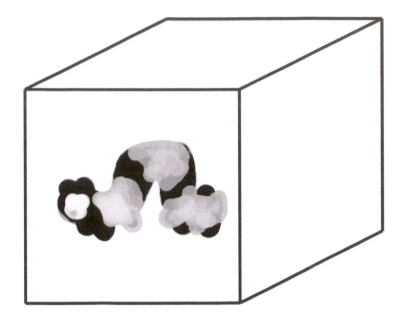

When the appropriate number of bugs have been collected they are put into the bags. But each bag can have no more than the number it has been given.

For some children you may want to illustrate what the number stands for and place the label flat. In this way children can picture-match the quantity and when the label is covered, the bugs and label can go in the bag together. In this case you can use the colour clue if it would help the child.

So far I have been talking about paper bags, but don't forget to look at plastic bags; they often have interesting and different pictures on them.

A few years ago a leading supermarket had a large Father Christmas on the side of their carrier bags. I did a lot of shopping in that shop so that I could get the bags! Carefully cut out the pictures or designs you want and either stick them on cardboard or, if possible, laminate them.

Use them for counting, hiding (use vocabulary to find them: above, below, under, through), developing a Santa trail or even creating a vertical number line.

Use bags that fit a theme. For instance, if you make Hungry Caterpillar games keep the playing pieces in a bag. Decorate the outside of the bag with caterpillar pictures so that children know which bag to collect to enable them to play the game. Using bags with handles means that they can be safely hung away until they are needed. This sometimes helps to keep all the pieces together!

Boxes

Cats love boxes: big boxes, small boxes, even items that resemble boxes, such as drawers, sinks and laundry baskets. Cats love boxes. Big cats, small cats, big boxes, small boxes – it doesn't seem to matter to the cats. Boxes are easy to get a hold of, are inexpensive and are often totally free.

My Cat Likes to Hide in Boxes by Eve Sutton is a good starting point.

What is a box? A very good question to get children talking. I usually put this in the context of an alien. Something like: 'I have just arrived here from another planet and my teacher has asked me to fetch a box. I don't know what that means. Tell me what I should look for. What does a box look like?'

It could be

 or

or

Encourage children to talk together, with their friend or with another adult. Some children will be able to visualise what a box is, others may need to fetch one and talk about that.

What do you think? Remember, if it's what a child thinks it cannot be wrong.

Just imagine what you could achieve if you thought you couldn't be wrong!

Do use actual boxes when you are talking about corners, edges or faces, so that the children have a visual image of what you are saying. Let them run their fingers along an edge and over a face to feel the difference.

Give each child or pair a toy cat and ask them to find a box that their cat will fit into. Is the box too big? Is it too small? Is it just right? You can use these as a small display with labels of too big, too small, just right.

Collect photos of real cats in boxes and sort them into the three categories:

- The cat is *too big* for the box.
- The box is *too big* for the cat.
- This box is *just right* for this cat.

The next stage after this is to ask the children to make a box for their cat and to test it. Is it too big, too small or just right?

Expect a huge range of boxes!

The Very Hungry Caterpillar

The Very Hungry Caterpillar is a children's picture book designed, illustrated and written by Eric Carle. It features a caterpillar that eats its way through a wide variety of foodstuffs before pupating and emerging as a butterfly.

What a lovely story for sequencing, learning the days of the week and the life cycle of a butterfly.

But what about taking the story a bit further?

Start collecting a variety of boxes which can be transformed into caterpillars. They can be any shape and any size.

Children can paint them, stick paper on them and make them their own.

As children gain more experience, offer them the choice of using two shades of green for the body and encourage them to experiment with different ways of covering their box. Some are shown below. They are examples of what some children have made and then played with. You can see they have been used well!

Let's take these caterpillars and develop the idea further.

Sort them into caterpillars that roll and those that don't. Or those with corners and those without. Or big caterpillars, small caterpillars. Wide and narrow, tall and short, fat and thin.

Next step? Make leaves for the caterpillars to eat through.

Use just one shape to start with; perhaps all the rectangles. Draw and cut a hole in the centre of the leaf. This hole should be almost the size of the caterpillar that you intend to go through it. (Smaller ones will go through, but not any larger ones.)

Ask the children to find the caterpillar that ate through each leaf and put that caterpillar on top of the leaf. Some smaller will be put through but this may mean that larger

ones are left which will not fit through the remaining holes. This gives opportunities for children to change their minds and try again.

HINT: When making the leaves use the same colour paper and the same shape and pattern around the edge. If you make them different the children will learn to match them by other means rather than looking at the size and shape of the hole. Not a bad thing but a totally different activity.

If you have caterpillars the same shape and size, they can be joined together by sticking Velcro patches at each end. Then you can ask children to make a long caterpillar, a short caterpillar, a caterpillar as long as your leg. The possibilities are endless.

And, as an aside, by placing the fruit that the caterpillar eats in a triangle, you get the pattern of triangle numbers! But that will be for another book!

Stacking boxes

These boxes are very easy to find, from charity shops to Harrods! And everything in between. Shoe shops are very willing to give you empty boxes ranging in size from large to baby size, so you are able to make your own set at no cost.

For younger children use no more than three or four, but for older children you can use up to twelve.

Show the children the boxes all hidden inside each other and ask: 'What can you see? Tell me something about what you can see.'

Respond to their answers with another question or by paraphrasing what they say in order to make it clearer to the other children. 'Yes, it is a box; can you tell me something else?' For example, colour, size, shape, corners/no corners and so on.

When all possibilites have been explored (or the children are fidgeting!) move to the next stage.

'Listen! What can you hear?' (Shake the box.) 'What do you think could be inside the box?'

A variety of answers could be given ranging from the optimistic 'sweets' to the more realistic 'a toy'. 'How can we find out?' *Don't* say 'We can take the lid off and find out.' It is better to let the children come up with their own suggestions.

If no-one mentions the lid, say: 'I wonder if we can take the lid off. Would we be able to see inside then?'

Taking the lid off needs to be full of tension mixed with excitement. Have a peek inside before you show the children, then slowly remove the lid and let them see. 'Another box!'

Place the first box where the children can see it and put the lid back on it.

Shake the boxes again and repeat as above to reveal the next box. Place this one next to the first one. 'How many boxes can we see?' Count the two on the table and the one in your hand. 'One, two, three boxes. I wonder if there are any more. Talk to your friend and tell them what you think. Are there going to be more boxes or is this one in my hand the last one?' Allow a minute for the children to talk. 'Who thinks this one in my hand is the last one? Who thinks there are some more? How can we find out?'

At this point you may get a very loud response of 'SHAKE THE BOX!'

Continue adding boxes to those already on the table, always counting them from one before you start with the next box. This will be a good reinforcement of early counting. When you know you have come to the last box, ask the questions again: 'Who thinks this one in my hand is the last one? Who thinks there are some more? How can we find out?'

Shake the box. 'What can you hear? Do you think this box is empty? Is it the last box? How can we find out?' You should get the response: 'TAKE THE LID OFF!'

Dice

Dice are throwable objects with multiple resting positions, used for generating random numbers. Dice are suitable for floor or tabletop games.

A traditional die is a rounded cube, with each of its six faces showing a different number of dots from one to six.

Sometimes they are small, sometimes they are large – but they don't always have what you would like on the faces.

Solution? Make your own!

The easiest way is to cover a box that is already a cube. How any times do you throw away your empty tissue boxes? Stop doing that at once!

Take out the tissues, store them in an empty cardboard box and get creative!

How about Incy Wincy Spider? You can find the rhyme in the next chapter. In order to move the spider up and down the drainpipe use a box covered in the weather symbols for rain and sun. Cover three faces with a rain symbol and three faces with a sun, and ask the children to take turns to throw the box. If the sun shows on the top, the spider moves up. If the rain shows, the spider moves down.

Using wrapping paper, cut out some bug pictures.

Either put one of each bug on the faces of the box die, or just start with two different ones.

Use 'The Ugly Bug Ball' or *The Bad-Tempered Ladybird* as possible starting points.

Children take turns to throw the box and collect a matching bug from an assorted pile on the floor. After five throws each see who has most of which bug.

Line them up in a one-to-one correspondence as shown below.

Player 1: 'I have three ladybirds.'
Player 2: 'I have four ladybirds. I have more ladybirds than you.'

Player 1: 'I have one caterpillar.'
Player 2: 'I have three caterpillars. I have more than you.'

For children who are still at the early stages of counting they can see who has most caterpillars by the pictures. The person with the longest line has most. The person with the shortest line has least. Once children are confident with the game, increase the number of different bugs.

Some tissue boxes have the same pictures on the faces of the box as on the tissues inside. A ready-made game!

Cover the top and bottom of the box with green paper for 'have another go' or red paper for 'miss a turn' or one of each.

Each player has a tissue, throws the box die and covers the matching picture. The first player to cover all their pictures is the winner. Or play without having a winner, just picture match and cover.

How simple is that for a game?

Or how about 'The Teddy Bears' Picnic'? You can use paper-bag puppets, cardboard-tube models or teddy-bear paper bags. Or make a number line with bears cut from wrapping paper.

'The Teddy Bears' Picnic' was written by John W. Bratton and Jimmy Kennedy. If you're not sure of the words or melody, you can find them online. Sing the song. Dance a happy dance. Have a picnic!

But back to the box die – how many teddy bears will be at the picnic today?

Use wrapping paper and cut out 21 small bears. Using one to six (or numbers suitable for the children) paste the bears onto the faces of the box to make a traditional 1–6 die, but with bears instead of spots.

Or you can arrange them in the pattern of traditional spot dice. All of maths is to do with pattern. Spot the pattern, apply it to another similar problem and you may well become quite a competent mathematician (and possibly musician). Children who don't see patterns may need a bit more support. So arranging the bears in the traditional way as on dice and dominoes may well help those who need it at a much earlier stage.

Children love to help you stick the bears on the box, or they can make their own to take home and play the game.

Use the rest of the bears from the paper as bears to be collected to sit round the picnic table.

Each child has a throw (if a large group) or three throws each (if a smaller group) and collects that number of cut-out bears to place around the picnic table.

Build a teddy-bear role-play area using actual teddy bears where they can sit on the chairs or benches. Get children to make real or dough food. Share the food equally among the bears. For example, twelve biscuits for six bears gives them two biscuits each. What if there were three bears or two bears, how many biscuits each then?

Set the scene on large paper or card. Stick the bears on with sticky patches which can be removed for the next game.

Or how about having a Teddy Bear Day?

Children can plan what they will need: food, music, games, clothes and much more. Give them a book to record what they need. Make some simple graphs to show who wants what. White bread or brown? Orange squash or water? Dancing music or a sing-along with music?

Let each child make a paper hat ready for the party. How can you measure around your head to make sure that the hats fits? That's a bit tricky! You may need a friend to help you.

Discuss (not tell!) different ways that this can be done. Show a range of hats, sort them into good party hats and not so good. Who wants to wear a knitted bobble hat to a party? (Actually, thinking about it, someone might!)

Make it their day, not yours! You are there to supply what is needed.

Children can write invitations to their family, make up a teddy-bear play using their puppets, cook teddy-bear shaped biscuits, bring their favourite teddy to school.

Oh, I wish I could be invited!

And it all started with a box!

Cardboard tubes

What exactly can you do with those leftover cardboard tubes? If you use kitchen roll and wrapping paper on a regular basis, then sooner or later you end up with a ton of leftover cardboard tubes – but don't toss them into the compost or recycling bin just yet (though they are actually very useful for aerating your compost).

Let's look at a few ideas and they will hopefully set you off on your own creative journey.

How about 'Ten in the Bed' (or 'Five in the Bed' for some children)? All you need is a boot box (or shoe box for 'Five in the Bed'), ten (or five) cardboard tubes and some Velcro. Any extras such as material for the bed are optional. Make sure that the tubes, when laid down, fit into the box.

I've always found that shoe shops are more than willing to give me empty boxes.

Paint or cover the box any colour. Stand the cardboard tubes upright and paint or cover in paper to make them look like people. Using material may make them unable to roll. Add cut paper for hair or a circle of paper for a hat.

While the people are drying, continue with the box. At one of the shorter ends cut a slit from the top to where it meets the base. Attach Velcro to each side of the cut so that the two pieces fold to close again.

Lay the people side by side in the box.

You have successfully completed the task and are now ready to share with the children. Sing or say the rhyme of 'Ten in the Bed'.

There were ten in the bed
And the little one said,
'Roll over, roll over.'
So they all rolled over and one fell out.
There were nine in the bed . . .

Depending on the tubes you used you may have had one that was shorter than the others, to be the little one. If, like me, you made them all the same size, stop after 'and the little one said' and say: 'We don't have a little one. What does it mean, a little one?'

This gives children the opportunity to discuss the meaning of the words big and little.

Exchange one of the people in the bed for a little one (one you have made earlier!) and continue with the rhyme. When it gets to the part where one of them falls out of bed, tip the box, open the Velcro and one will fall out. Make sure you're quick to close it again or you may find that they all tumble out!

You may want to count the ones that have fallen out and count the ones still in the bed. Or you can put numbers on them and link ordinal and cardinal numbers so that number 1 is the first to fall out, number 2 is the second and so on. Or for older or more able children make number 10 the first to fall out and the number on the next one (9) tells us how many are still left in the box.

How about using the tubes for a dinosaur landscape?

Or an ice city:

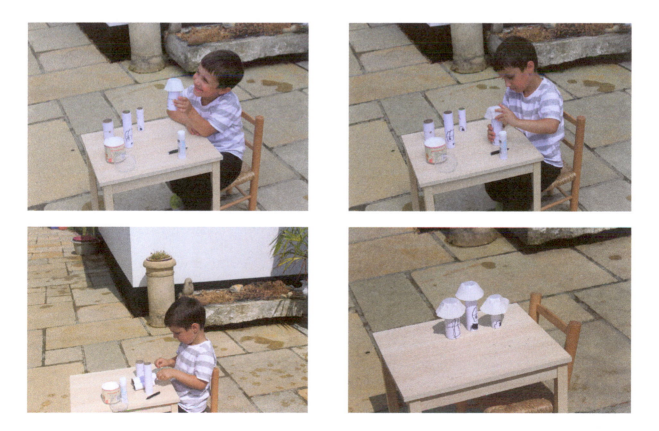

Stand the buildings on a silver cake board, sprinkle silver glitter all over everything and you have one happy child, an empty glitter tube and a mess that takes weeks to completely clear.

Mobiles

A mobile is a type of sculpture constructed to take advantage of the principle of balance. It can consist of a number of rods, from which weighted objects or further rods hang. The objects hanging from the rods balance each other, so that the rods remain more or less horizontal. Each rod hangs from only one string, which gives it freedom to rotate about the string.

To make a simple mobile you will need a coat hanger, some string and cardboard tubes.

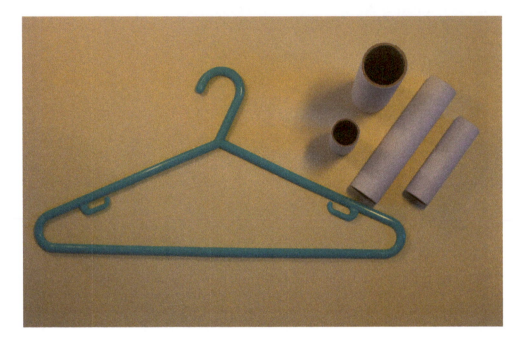

Decide on the theme for your mobile. Link it with a story maybe. Winnie-the-Pooh and his bees come to mind.

A. A. Milne named the character Winnie-the-Pooh after a teddy bear owned by his son, Christopher Robin Milne, who was the basis for the character Christopher Robin. In the first chapter of *Winnie-the-Pooh*, Milne offers this explanation of why Winnie-the-Pooh is often called simply 'Pooh':

> But his arms were so stiff . . . they stayed up straight in the air for more than a week, and whenever a fly came and settled on his nose he had to blow it off. And I think – but I am not sure – that that is why he is always called Pooh.

As with the caterpillars before, allow the children to experiment with painting their own bees. Be prepared for a variety of offerings! But, as I have said before, and will no doubt say again, if it's what the children think their bee should look like, it cannot be wrong!

Younger children may need help with attaching the string. But don't make the decision for them about where this should be. They may want a bee that appears to be plummeting to the ground, or flying to the sky. It's their decision, not yours.

Story bags, story boxes and story-telling

A story bag or sack is a bag containing a book, plus items associated with the story, which might include characters in the form of soft toys or puppets. There might also be a non-fiction book on a similar theme; this allows children to experience different types of text. These items are used to help bring the story to life.

You can make your own story bag – or it could be a box – and include whatever you feel is appropriate for the children who will be using it.

Involve others in creating these bags or boxes and let families take them home to share with their children.

Collect ideas from other cultures about stories that can be developed.

The bag

You don't need a fancy bag to make a story sack! Even a simple paper bag will do. Just decorate the outside of the bag, fill it with the book and other related objects and you're ready to go. What the bag looks like doesn't matter too much, although you do want it to look inviting to the child. It is what's inside the bag that counts.

The story

What story book you pick will depend on the child (or children) you are making it for.

If the story sack is for a specific child, you might want to take into account any special interests or favourite characters that the child likes. For example, you might not want to pick out a story about birds if the child loves tigers! The more interested the child is in the subject of the story, the more likely they will be to read and truly enjoy the book.

Filling the bag

With some stories, the possibilities are endless for related crafts, games, etc. With others, you will have to get a bit more creative. Here are some ideas to help you decide what to put in the sack with the story book:

- Supplies to make related puppets, games, props, costumes, etc.
- A CD or tape of the story being told
- A fact book to learn more about situations or items in the story
- A purchased game or toy that is related to the story
- Pictures of related places or events
- Plain paper and crayons to write or draw a story
- Written suggestions and items to help act out the story
- Objects related to the story
- Related videos to watch.

Handy hints

Bags

Oher than polythene, any type of bag can be used. Big ones, small ones, paper ones, gift bags, tall ones, plain ones, sparkly ones.

Have a large box filled with various materials for children to use. Paper bags can be used for making a road, filling with blocks, wearing as gloves, making hats. Fostering creativity means accepting new ways of using things or of using materials.

Use empty paper bags or boxes to make a number line. You will need eleven bags, coloured pens, scissors and glue. Use the markers to draw an outline on one side of the bag of a building that the children see regularly. It could be a shop, post office, house, school, fire station, restaurant and so on. Use stickers to represent windows that show zero to ten. Stick them on using the pattern of spots found on dice or dominoes. On the other side add a door that has a numeral 0–10 (or 0–5 if that is more appropriate).

Line the bags/boxes up in a random order. Challenge children to find the bag/box with a specific number. Then check with the number on the door.

Ask children to line the bags/boxes in the correct numerical order, or odd and even numbers.

Use small-world play models to fill the bag/box with the correct number of items.

Boxes

Large boxes in or out of doors are open invitations to a child's creativity. They can become caves, rockets, aeroplanes, homes or trucks. They can become anything that the children want to imagine. Don't be too quick to make suggestions; wait and see what happens.

Cardboard tubes

Once you have some cardboard tubes, you and the children are ready to get started on lots of different projects:

- Make binoculars for intrepid explorers. Use them to spot something long; short; blue; square.
- Make animals by poking holes for legs, use straws for the legs, and decorate. Make a jungle. Make a farm.

Involve parents and carers

As always, safety must be carefully considered before introducing any materials.

Run workshops for parents, with their children if possible, to pass on the following important messages. But first ask yourself:

- Do you encourage children to use materials in unconventional ways?
- Do you provide materials that stimulate creativity and imaginative play?
- Do you actively encourage children to talk about and describe what they are doing and what they are feeling?

If you do, then pass that on! It is very valuable!

As a teacher I always said that I was going to publish a colouring book that fostered creativity. It would have colourful covers and inside there would be twenty completely blank pages!

Although there is a place for books with pictures already drawn on the pages, they have very little flexibility and 'tell' children what to do. Unfortunately they do not have anything to do with fostering original thought and creativity.

Maths games

Games are a fun way to engage children in maths.

On the Farm: You will need: paper bags, marker, plastic farm animals.

Write a different number on the outside of each bag. One player has a handful of animals, the other has the bag. (Adjust according to how many players there are.)

Each player with a bag needs to get the correct number of animals from the 'animal' player by asking for one or two at a time. They cannot get more than the number on a bag. After all the bags have been filled, players switch roles and play again.

Five Little Monkeys: Use an empty shoebox and five toys to consolidate subtraction. Introduce the rhyme 'Five little monkeys jumping on the bed'.

Five little monkeys jumping on the bed,
One fell off and bumped his head.
The doctor came and the doctor said
'No more monkeys jumping on the bed!'

Four little monkeys jumping on the bed,
One fell off and bumped his head . . .

until there are no more monkeys jumping on the bed. Change 'monkeys' to the toy that is being used.

Chapter 3: Hair-related items

This chapter looks at how hair-related items (hairbands, hair scrunchies and shower caps) can be used to help children's communication and language, maths and vocabulary. It includes familiar rhymes and activities using both the teacher's and child's creativity.

Below are the main learning objectives for the following activities.

Communication and language

Listening and attention: Children listen attentively in a range of situations. They listen to stories, accurately anticipating key events, and respond to what they hear with relevant comments, questions or actions.

Understanding: Children follow instructions involving several ideas or actions. They answer 'how' and 'why' questions about their experiences and in response to stories or events.

Vocabulary

Counting and recognising numbers:
Number
Zero, one, two, three . . . to twenty and beyond
Count, count (up) to
Count back (from, to)
Count in ones
Position, direction and movement:
Position
Above, below
Top, bottom
Before, after
Between
Direction
Up, down
Forwards, backwards
Along
Movement

Mathematics

Numbers: Children count reliably with numbers from one to twenty, place them in order and say which number is one more or one less than a given number.

Shape, space and measures: Children use everyday language to talk about position and to solve problems. They explore characteristics of everyday objects and shapes and use mathematical language to describe them.

Hairbands or hair scrunchies

Hairbands and hair scrunchies are used to wrap around a ponytail or bun for an instant, glamorous look.

Language and maths are important tools that allow humans to better understand the world around them, and communicate with one another. Many times children are taught to read and write mathematics before they understand the concepts. One way to help develop this understanding is to use visual, tactile and interesting materials such as hair scrunchies or hairbands, which will not only get the attention of children, but also keep their concentration.

This section will look at just one way of engaging young children, or those who still struggle in the later years, with the concept of a number line. (There's more about number lines in Chapter 4.) Very early in their school life, children are expected to be competent users of number lines of different types to help with mental calculation and therefore develop a mental image to carry with them throughout their subsequent years.

Incy Wincy Spider and friends

Let me take you through the journey of Incy Wincy Spider and his friends.

Incy Wincy Spider climbed up the waterspout.
Down came the rain and washed the spider out.
Out came the sun and dried up all the rain.
Incy Wincy Spider climbed up the spout again.

This is one version of the popular nursery rhyme that describes the adventures of a spider as it goes up, comes down, goes up and comes down the downspout or 'waterspout' of a gutter system as many times as you sing the song. It is sometimes accompanied by the children making the actions of the spider by moving their hands and fingers.

How about this?

What do we need? A spider.

What else? A drainpipe and a spout to fix on the end.

The children use a length of pipe lagging as their own drainpipe. This is much easier to handle than a traditional drainpipe, which can be quite heavy. It also takes away the possibility of injury as children carry the drainpipes through the classroom area. One lapse of concentration can leave a nasty round mark on another child! There is also, of course (drawn from an experience which I won't go further into), the possibility of the drainpipes being used as swords as soon as your back is turned. Hard plastic can draw blood! Much better to use pipe lagging or bendy swimming aids to stop that happening. They don't even leave a tiny red mark!

There are many options for a spider. I used a hair scrunchy which can be washed when needed. Through my experience of working with young children I often find, on arriving home, that some of my resources feel decidedly damp. That's not too bad, but I want to know the reason for the dampness. The best answer is to always use washable or laminated materials!

But you could make one as part of class activities using paper plates, pom-poms with added pipe cleaners or even drawings from the children attached to a rubber band. Or use a cardboard tube, paint it spider-colour and make cuts up the lower part for legs. (Remember! Spiders have eight legs, not six.) Stick or paint eyes at the top and use an elastic band to attach it to the drainpipe.

As an aside, try making spiders using Oreo biscuits and liquorice or Matchmakers for legs. Delicious! But maybe just for the staffroom.

Introduce the spider and the drainpipe to the class. Discuss the meaning of drainpipes, and why we need them. You may want to go on a drainpipe hunt outside. You could even set up an outside spider role-play area. Provide different lengths and types of pipe, a large jug of water, and see what happens as children pour the water from the jug down through the pipe.

Place the spider at the bottom of the drainpipe. Sing the song all together and as the children sing move the spider up the spout, providing a very powerful visual connection between the word 'up' and the action. When the children sing the word 'down' the spider moves down the drainpipe, which again gives a very strong visual image.

This can be repeated as many or as few times that the time allocated or the attention of the audience allows.

A smaller version of the drainpipe (pipe lagging) and spare spiders can be placed in the book corner or in a role-play area of stories and rhymes, so that the children can make it a child-initiated activity rather than it always being a teacher-led one.

Moving on

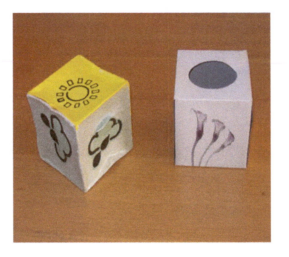

After a while, this activity can lose its appeal, so we need to move it on a step. Using an empty tissue box, involve the children in making different dice which can be used with this rhyme. The one shown on the left of the picture has three faces with the symbol for the sun and three faces with the symbol of rain.

Start the spider in the centre of the drainpipe and ask children to take turns to throw the die and decide, according to the picture shown, whether the spider is to move up or down. Encourage the children to interpret the data themselves and to base their decision on their knowledge of the rhyme. (Try not to tell them the answer. They only learn to wait for you before answering!) They can ask a friend to help and they can change their mind.

A problem can arise if, for instance, the spider is moved upwards, to the very top of the drainpipe, and the next player throws a sun. What can we do now? *Don't* make the decision for the children. Ask 'I wonder what we can do about this. There is nowhere for the spider to move to. What do you think we can do about this?' Accept all of their thoughts and act on them. If you ask the children to give a solution to a problem, you must give them the respect of trying it out as a solution. If you don't want to do it, don't ask them! Once you have passed the problem to the class, it is their problem, not yours. Asking children 'what do you think?' means that they cannot be wrong! Our skill as the teacher is to take what they think and move it (if necessary) to where we want them to be.

Keep moving

Again, after a while, we need to move the activity on to the next stage for those who are ready. Make a mark at regular intervals on the drainpipe, using any coloured tape. The pipe can then be used as a vertical number line where the numbers will be written on the lines (with no numbers yet!), or a vertical number track where the numbers will be written in the spaces between the marks. Start the spider in the middle as before, take turns to throw the die, but this time the spider is moved up or down only one mark or space. So it will go to the one above or the one below. Once the spider has reached the very top or the very bottom, the game ends and, if there is time, another one can be started.

The last stage is to put numbers on the marks or in the spaces (always include a zero), so that we can talk about 'four is one more than three' or 'five is one less than six'. Moving on again, the numbers can be any that you want to use. Don't always start with zero, use multiples of two; you could even go into negative numbers.

What else?

Are you tired of the spider? Find other hair scrunchies to use. Those shown are a very small part of my collection! Any story or rhyme where there is movement up and down can be used: Hickory Dickory Dock; Jack and the Beanstalk; Rapunzel; Jack and Jill; The Grand Old Duke of York, and so on.

It would be nonsense to move the giraffe up a vertical number line, although it could move along a horizontal one. If you want to use it vertically, undo the seam in the neck and stitch in shirring elastic. That is about the thinnest elastic you can find and stretches very well.

For the giraffe, you could use a 1, 2, 3, 1, 2, 3 box die and leaves. Stand the giraffe at zero and as the die is thrown, stretch the neck up to that number and collect the leaves, where one leaf is on the number 1, two leaves are on the number 2, and so on.

Teaching tip: Always replace the leaves ready for the next player, who may throw the same number. Each player has, for example, five turns each of throwing and collecting. The winner is the player with most leaves. For those children who may still find counting a challenge, use one-to-one correspondence to find the longest line of leaves. Another teaching tip: make all the leaves the same size or this part won't work.

If you can't find a suitable scrunchy, make your own or set it as a parent/child task at home.

Once the up and down has become very familiar and the children show great understanding of the vertical number line (don't forget your height chart, and a thermometer or the scales on the side of jugs) turn the drainpipe (now without the spout on the end) to make a horizontal line. Use hairbands or dolls with a band round them to repeat the activity but moving from left to right. Use unnumbered lines first to reinforce the left to right movement.

For example, the cow moves towards the cowshed, the sheep moves to the field, the dinosaur to the cave, the dog to the kennel and so on. Draw or ask children to draw the home of each animal and attach it to the end of the drainpipe.

Put different pictures on the box die to allow the 'animal' to move to the right as well as to the left.

One particularly popular idea with older children is to have the box painted in the colours of two different football teams. Or it can be the colours of the school football team and an opposing school team.

For this activity I use a small finger puppet attached to the pipe with a hairband. The class is divided into two teams and each team takes turns to throw the die. If the colours of their team show on top the 'player' moves one line or space towards the goal. If it shows the colours of the opposing team, they don't move at all. Play continues until one team reaches the end and 'scores' a goal. Play the best of three matches. I would suggest that no player has to move backwards towards the start. This could mean that one game lasts a week! Even I get fed up by then!

Shower caps

This section looks at how shower caps can be used to help children's communication and language, maths and vocabulary, as well as developing their creativity. It includes activities that use familiar rhymes as a starting point, but can be extended on to other stories.

Simple travel shower caps can be bought quite cheaply from chemists and usually come in packs of three or five. Be aware that they are made of plastic so children need to be supervised when using them.

This must be my best idea ever! And it all came about by a wonderful chance discovery.

As usual I was spending time rummaging through other people's donations in a local charity shop, when I uncovered the most amazing shower cap.

I hadn't a clue why I wanted it; it certainly wasn't to wear in the shower. For me, having a shower is all about washing my hair, so no shower cap needed there!

But I had to buy it; I had a voice in my head that said 'It may be useful one day.'

And thank goodness I did. Over the next few months I managed to find other caps that fitted the same theme. Not all from charity shops, but from supermarkets or chemists.

And then, delight of all delights, I found a bag to keep them in. (That was another charity-shop buy, twenty pence. Bargain!)

Now, what to do with them?

I shall take you through my journey.

The house in which I live has a large inglenook fireplace with a small step up to go into it. We often use it as a makeshift stage. While singing and playing with my grand-children, we took turns to sing our favourite nursery rhyme, standing on our stage.

These nursery rhymes gradually evolved into a play that the boys wanted to develop, but what to do about costumes?

This was my light-bulb moment.

Farm animals were needed. And what did I have in my bag?

The farm animals were all ready to be used. The boys were quickly kitted out (at this time of writing I have six grandsons, but another baby is on the way, so, who knows?) and the play began. Unfortunately the youngest wanted to be a dinosaur! (More about this later.) However, we made a paper-bag hat and he was ready to go. The play was duly 'written', rehearsed and executed and a good time was had by all.

But would this work in an early years setting? There was only one way to find out. So off I went to a very friendly nursery and I was allowed to develop the idea there.

This is what happened:

'Let's sing "Old MacDonald Had a Farm" and when we come to the part "and on that farm he had a . . . " you choose which animal you want to be. Close your eyes and think of an animal. Are you all ready? Have you got an animal in your head? Then let's go.'

We all sing, pause, add the animal noise and sing some more.

'That was really good. But your animals were very quiet. We'll do it again and you can really shout the sound your animal makes. Ready? Let's go!'

We all sing, pause, ADD THE ANIMAL NOISE (wow, that was loud) and sing some more.

'My goodness, what noisy animals there are on the farm. This time you all shouted so loudly, I couldn't really hear what sounds you made. What do you think we can do about that? Can you think of another way that I can get to know which animal you chose?'

Give time for children to think and talk to the person next to them. Accept all answers, value their responses. Some ideas that may come are:

Draw a picture (not always helpful. Many a mouse has closely resembled an elephant, but I did have the picture upside down!)
Hold an animal from the small play farm
Hold up a soft toy
Use sign language.

Get into groups of the same animal. (One child suggested the animals with legs get in one set and the animals with no legs get into a different set. Tricky when you're looking at farm animals!)

One of the problems with 'What do you think?' is that you will never know in advance what the children *will* think! But accept all answers and try them out. This may take some time so plan it over a few hours or a few days. But I strongly believe that if you have asked a child for an idea and then you ignore it, eventually that child will stop offering any thoughts at all. We're trying to build confidence and self-esteem, so let's show some respect!

Lecture over! Back to the shower caps.

'I have an idea. I have something in my bag that can help us choose the animals. Shall we use that idea?' I introduce my idea right at the end of trying out child-initiated ideas.

Out comes my bag of shower caps.

'We'll sing the song up until "and on that farm there was a . . . " and I will choose someone to take something out of my bag.'

There was mainly excitement but some trepidation, especially among the adults, who had no idea what was in the bag!

Off we go! With enthusiastic but not necessarily tuneful singing we reached the part of the song when the animal appears. All of a sudden a strange thing happened. The whole class sat up straight and folded their arms with one finger pointing up covering their lips! I always smile when that happens. I wonder who started that and how many years ago it was.

Choose a child from this class of perfection to take a hat from the bag without looking inside, and ask them to tell you what the animal is. They can then put it on their head or hold it if they are a little shy.

Continue singing and choosing and wearing until all of the hats have gone.

There will be great disappointment amongst the children who are still waiting to choose. Play the game a few more times until most, if not all, have managed to have a turn if they want to. Some may not.

As I drove home from the nursery I had another

Out came my empty tissue boxes and I made a box die of the animals that we had used plus an extra one. Do you remember the dinosaur from my grandson's play? I found one!

I put the five farm animals and the dinosaur on my box ready to take next time. Now to work out how to bring a dinosaur into a farm.

This is how it went next time:

'I really enjoyed the animal hats we used last time, did you?' ('Yes.') 'I would like to play the game again, would you?' ('Yes.') 'I have an extra surprise this time.'

Off we went again, singing, choosing, wearing and singing again until all of the hats had gone from the bag. But this time I left out the dinosaur hat and had previously hidden it in the classroom.

I produced the box die and explained that the children wearing the hats would keep wearing them until someone threw the die and looked at the picture on the top. They would then go to the person wearing that hat, say 'Please can I have the sheep/dog/cat/cow?' and the child wearing it would happily pass it over. Don't have high hopes of this happening first, second or even (with some children) the twentieth time. Either the taking child snatches the hat off the head (sometimes taking some hair with it), or the giving child hangs on to the legs. But this is all part of producing a child with social skills and manners, so persevere!

I usually ask the group to sit in a ring so that they don't have to climb over anyone when collecting a hat. As they stand up they move around the outside of the ring. Growing in confidence as they play, children are getting up, moving to where they need to be and sitting back down at an alarming rate. Shyer children can take a friend with them.

But let's move on to the next development.

At the end of a very robust game I asked 'How many pigs did we have and how many cows?' Of course no-one had kept count. The children were far too excited and the adults were far too anxious about noise and health and safety issues. HINT: Play the game outside on grass if possible.

I had made a set of picture cards that matched the pictures on the die. So now when the children played the game they collected the hat and also a matching picture card. In this way they still had the picture even when the hat had been given away.

But what of the dinosaur?

My secret weapon! When the children threw the die, they collected the matching animal. But when the dinosaur was thrown they were sent to look for the matching hat (hidden in the classroom, if you remember). This had to be done under controlled conditions with children following quite specific instructions. This was a good opportunity to practise our direction words: 'Go through, look up or look down. Look next to or beside. Look inside or outside. Look over, look under' and so on.

When the dinosaur was found and the child was wearing it, all the other animals came back into the bag, hiding from the dinosaur. This effectively ended the game. *But* because of the chance nature of the game, the dinosaur could be the first or the ninety-first throw. Have plenty of matching cards available!

But what use are the cards? I will tell you.

After all the animals were back in the bag, the children looked at the cards that they had and drew a picture of Old MacDonald's farm. They could have the farmer, some barns and a few tractors but the only animals they could have were the ones they had collected. What a perfect data-handling activity. They could arrange the cards in any way, so, for example, they could have all of the cows together or a couple of cows and a dog, with the other cows being in a different field. The choice was the children's. As long as they drew the right number of each animal according to their cards that was fine by me.

For older children who can work with bigger amounts, have two or three children putting their cards together so that they now have to draw even more. Don't get bogged down with colouring them in. Use colours as the outlines but send them home to be coloured. Or use a wet playtime.

Older children may like to use their pictures to develop a pictogram or a simple bar chart. If they do, ask them to tell you what they know about the number of each animal and how they know it. It could be counting or there may be a numbered axis. Ask questions such as 'Which animal do you have most/least of on your farm? How many sheep/cows? The farmer wants just eight animals; how many ways can he make eight?' Change the number according to the number of animals on the graph.

If you are not lucky enough to find your shower caps in shops, look online. Put 'animal shower caps' into your search engine and there they will be. All sorts.

What if you don't want to pay for them? (Join the club!) Then how about a hotel that leaves them in your bathroom? Some hotels may be willing to give you a small supply – or you can stay for a couple of nights and get your own! Perhaps you could get all the guests along your corridor to push theirs under your door.

Give the children their own shower cap to decorate. The designs they produce can be free choice, or you may want a set to fit in with a theme or a story.

Safety warning: Make sure there is an adult nearby as a child may put a shower cap over their face. Pierce some holes in the caps before use.

Safety tip: Make sure the glue is dry before the caps are put on heads; painful to get off otherwise.

I'm still developing ideas around these shower caps. I'm sure there are many more. I may get a whole new set of other animals and make a zoo! There are lots of rhymes and stories around the idea of a zoo.

Moral of this story: Listen to children. They have wonderful things to say!

Hints and tips

Be aware of safety issues when children are using shower caps when making their own animal hats.

If children are using glue, make sure that it is on the outside of the hat, otherwise there may be a problem getting the hat off the child's head.

Make the hats a few days before you want to use them. This allows the glue to dry and any glitter, etc, to fall off before wearing.

Involve parents and carers

Have a fun making session for the family. Give ideas of stories or rhymes where the caps can be used.

Don't just make animals. How about aliens, minibeasts or robots?

Chapter 4: Number lines

This chapter looks at the development of number lines, from those with no numbers to those with numbers. Writing numbers on a number line makes it easy to tell which numbers are bigger or smaller.

Numbers on the left are smaller than numbers on the right. This remains true when working in only positive or in positive and negative numbers.

We can use the number line to help us add. We always move to the right to add.

We can use the number line to help us subtract. We always move to the left to subtract.

When using a vertical number line we move up to add and down to subtract.

A number line is a continuous line representing numbers. It is a visual image which will help children to understand our number system. It can be used from the Foundation Stage upwards, and can help to teach addition and subtraction, counting in regular steps, and seeing the pattern of multiplication and division, as well as reinforcing ordinal and cardinal numbers.

The following activities use familiar stories and rhymes as a starting point to introduce young children to the concept of a number line.

Below are the main learning objectives for the following activities.

Communication and language

Development: Involves giving children opportunities to experience a rich language environment; to develop their confidence and skills in expressing themselves; and to speak and listen in a range of situations.

Understanding: Children follow instructions involving several ideas or actions. They answer 'how' and 'why' questions about their experiences and in response to stories or events.

Speaking: Children express themselves effectively, showing awareness of listeners' needs. They use past, present and future forms accurately when talking about events that have happened or are to happen in the future. They develop their own narratives and explanations.

Mathematics

Involves providing children with opportunities to develop and improve their skills in counting, understanding and using numbers, and calculating simple addition and subtraction problems.

Numbers: Children count reliably with numbers from one to twenty, place them in order and say which number is one more or one less than a given number. Using quantities and objects, they add and subtract two.

Vocabulary

Number, one, two . . . ten

How many?

Count, first, second . . . tenth

Before, after, beside, next to, between

The empty number line

This is an empty number line. It is extremely useful and important for developing children's mathematics as well as their thinking. It can be oriented in any direction.

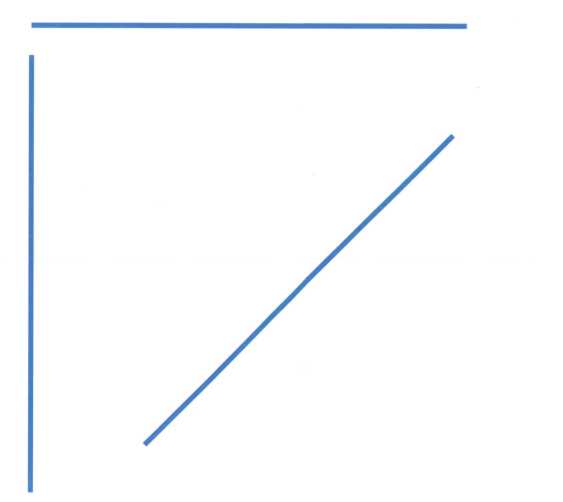

The line has no markings or scale; it does not need to be drawn neatly with a ruler. It does not even matter which way up it is. The power of the empty number line lies in its ability to provide an image or picture of a calculation or a position of a numeral which can develop children's thinking about the structure of numbers, and enable them to move on from simply counting on in ones.

But, before children can begin to use an empty number line, do they need to have had lots of experience of counting on and back using numbered lines, bead strings and partly numbered lines?

I think not. What if we start with the empty number line and then gradually, over time, add the numbers?

Developing a mental image

When children are used to using the empty number line, both vertical and horizontal, with the later addition of numbers it can help to improve their knowledge and understanding of the position of numbers compared with other numbers as well as their mental calculations, by providing a picture in their minds (a mental image), so eventually they might not need to draw a line to help them; they are using one mentally.

The empty number line is flexible in that it can be drawn on paper quickly and easily anywhere, and can eventually be used to represent an infinite range of numbers, including decimals. It is an excellent way for children to record their mathematical thinking; it can be used effectively by young children who are just beginning to record their mathematics, through to older pupils needing a calculation method for subtraction involving decimals. It shows children's thinking, knowledge and understanding about numbers. It allows them to show pictorially what they are doing and how they are doing it. But it has to have its beginnings as soon as possible so that there is time to use and understand the workings of such a powerful piece of equipment.

Using familiar rhymes and stories is a good start.

Nine hairy monsters

Nine hairy monsters came to school today.
Boo said the teacher and one ran away.
Dong went the bell and the children came to play
With eight hairy monsters in the playground, in the playground.
Eight hairy monsters came to school today . . . .

Continue until you have no hairy monsters.

At the beginning, let the children take the part of the monsters. Start with fewer, maybe three or five.

When one monster runs away, the child sits down and joins the rest of the group.

When the teacher says 'BOO' all the group join in.

If you have an old school bell or can get one from your music cupboard, give the responsibility of the 'Dong' to a child.

This is a very simple activity where all you need to do is to count to three initially. No writing, no numbers to put in order, just saying the words in order. They can be linked to amounts later. After one of the monsters has gone, start counting from the first one so that it reinforces the sound of the number names.

None left!

Gradually increase the number of monsters used until you reach nine. Repeat the activity above in exactly the same way.

I was browsing round the market and saw a huge amount of fur fabric at discount prices. I struck a bargain, which involved the purchase of a burger and some chips (not for me!), and bought a large amount of material. Now, what to do with it?

My husband wasn't keen on fur fabric cushions or loo seat covers or even a waistcoat. This was just as well, as I evolved a plan.

Using a very simple pattern, i.e. none, I cut the shapes and stitched them together to make the hairy monster shapes. These were then stuffed with hypo-allergenic stuffing which was also washable. The felt eyes were firmly stitched to make them as safe as possible for mouthing children.

Safety tip: Make sure the children using them do not have any fur or feather allergy.

Teaching tip: Check the bulge under a sweatshirt at home time. You may have to start with eight monsters tomorrow!

The children were each given a monster and asked to stand side by side. A bit of shuffling and movement got the children in a different order. So instructions like, 'blue stand next to red'; 'yellow stand between orange and green'; 'white stand next to green', and so on, would be good. Lovely for using positional language which later the children began to use.

The activity took place many times (I think the favourite part was being able to shout 'BOO!') and the children never got tired of it, but it was time to move on.

During one session I changed the furry monsters for pictures of furry monsters. The colours used were the same as before.

We used these for a long time. Sometimes the children chose the furry monsters, sometimes the pictures and sometimes some of each. The only rule for that was that no colour could be repeated. This made it easier when putting children in different positions.

Eventually, when the children were ready, I added the numerals. Each picture monster had a number on the reverse that only the child could see. This didn't work too well! So, I kept those numbers there but added drop-down numbers as well. These were attached by treasury tags.

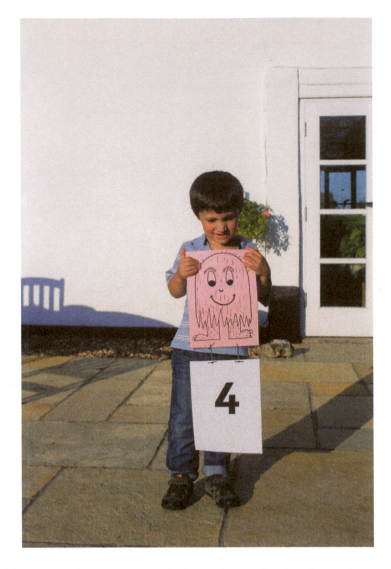

The nine children stood in a row, side by side, with the drop-down numbers shown in order.

Over time I changed this to standing in a random order. When we reached this stage, the rest of the class took turns to ask the children to move to a new place, such as:

'Clare stand next to Jon.'

'Vicki stand between Oliver and Thomas.'

'James and Stephen stand next to each other.'

And so on to make a traditional number line of monsters. After each move we counted together the numbers starting from the left-hand end.

Sometimes one part of the line was in order but not another part, so we had discussions about what number we should start with. For the furry monsters we started with one, as holding a monster with zero attached didn't make sense. How could you have no monsters when you were plainly holding one?!

Once the numerals were in order we began. This can be played in two ways. Either the first monster to go is number 1, so linking ordinal or cardinal numbers (as with 'Ten in the Bed') or 9 could go first leaving 8 at the end, showing how many monsters were left.

Sometimes, as children became more confident, a monster was randomly chosen to go, and the children had to say which numeral was missing. This became quite difficult for some, as they were now being asked to use mental imagery. Having a number line on the wall helped!

Some children were given a table-top number line that showed how the pattern of adding one more grew.

1. 2. 3.

1. 2.

1.

Frog beanbags

Beanbags can be easily made from any material but I rather liked one with frogs.

Most, if not all, young children meet the 'Five Little Speckled Frogs' at some time in their early years. And this fabric fitted the theme so well. There was a special offer at the shop so I got free lining material with it.

The first thing was to make the beanbags out of the lining and some washed pea gravel from the garden. Weighted beanbags are easier to throw and don't just flop on the ground. I used different amounts of gravel for each frog in a set so that we could talk about heaviest, heavier than, lightest and lighter than. The pea gravel was encased in some wadding to stop the sharpness coming through; the whole thing was stitched three times round the edges using a sewing machine.

Now for the frogs. I used two of the same frog for each beanbag. I stitched them inside out to make a pouch. After turning them the right way the pea gravel bag was popped inside and the open edge was stitched. I made five of each design.

The children sat in a ring with a long rope making a circle in front of them. Each child was given one frog and they took it in turns to throw it into the 'pool' (skipping rope ring).

We started singing:

Five little speckled frogs
Sitting on a speckled log
Eating their nice delicious grubs, yum yum.
One jumped into the pool
Where it was nice and cool
And that left just four speckled frogs glug glug.

And as we got to the part of 'One jumped into the pool' the children took turns to throw their frogs.

When the last one had 'jumped' we collected the frogs that didn't quite make it and counted the ones that did. Each was matched with an identical frog picture made from leftover material and laminated. Sticking the material on card would do just as well. (Material permitting; you need to make a lot of these. There is no need to make them double-sided, as only one side will be seen.)

We made a simple pictogram to see how many frogs made it the first three times we played. We played the game three times and each time added to the pictogram using frogs that matched those in the pool. We talked about the frogs that made it and those that didn't. We used the pictogram as a simple no-number number line by talking about the longest and shortest rows of frogs, where the longest means most and the shortest means least.

Some children, who were able to, counted the frogs in each row and, if appropriate, added a numeral to the end.

I must admit that the throwing improved over time. Not many children ended up with a frog on their head or in their lap.

Now was the time to increase the number of frogs.

Each child now had five frogs, all of the same design.

The song went as before until 'One jumped into the pool' and then each child threw one frog, so the possible total in the pool was five. (This didn't happen often at the beginning, but it did get better.)

We carried on until the end of the song. Now this was the tricky part. Some children forgot which design was their frog so were tempted to collect a lot more from the pool than they should have done. A two-year-old ran off clutching an armful of frogs and tried to hide them in his toddle truck. A great time was had by all!

The next time we played, each child was given one of the laminated pictures from the leftover material that matched their design. This made collecting frogs a lot easier and more successful, as all the children were asked to do was to match their picture to the one on the frogs.

As before, we made simple pictograms but this time using the different designs of frog to see which the best jumper was. It's important to let children know that this is not a race or a competition. The results may well be different next time when different people are involved in the throwing.

Pastry and biscuit cutters

These are usually found in every kitchen in the land and, we hope, in a lot of early years settings. They come in all shapes, sizes and colours.

When you make dough or pastry or biscuits, talk about the biggest, smallest, most, least. Ask questions such as: 'If chocolate is your favourite biscuit, would you like this one' (*show the largest cutter*) 'or this one?' (*show the smallest cutter*). 'Why did you choose that one?' Then: 'If we made worm biscuits would you like this one or this one?' Some children will say the biggest, but that's inevitable! Always ask why.

'Let's make biscuits for the three bears. We need a big one for Daddy Bear, a small one for Baby Bear and a middle size one for Mummy Bear.' (Although in my house it's always Mummy who gets the biggest!) 'How many biscuits do we have?'

Match the biscuits with pictures or teddy bears. What if Baby Bear has a friend to play? How many now?

Flowers on hooks

Mary, Mary, quite contrary
How does your garden grow?
With silver bells and cockle shells
And pretty maids all in a row.

'Mary, Mary, Quite Contrary' is a popular English nursery rhyme. The rhyme has been seen as having religious and historical significance, but its origins and meaning are disputed. Like many nursery rhymes, it has acquired various historical explanations.

The oldest known version was first published in *Tommy Thumb's Pretty Song Book* (*c*.1744) with the following lyrics:

Mistress Mary, Quite contrary,
How does your garden grow?
With Silver Bells, And Cockle Shells,
And so my garden grows.

But whatever the origin, many people have fond memories of the rhyme from when they were young.

While perusing a well-known shop of Swedish origin I found, in the basement, some wooden flowers.

Not sure that I would like them in my house, I knew that there would be a use for them at some time in the future, so I bought ten. They went into my already bulging trolley. Continuing my walk, I arrived in the picture frame/useful hooks section. Thank goodness I did. For there, in a bargain bin, was the very thing that I didn't even know I was looking for.

I had found the reason for my flowers. A perfect match.

I couldn't wait to get back home and try my idea with the ever-patient grandchildren, and then, if successful, launch it into my friendly nursery and beyond.

Children were given the flowers to hold and as we sang the rhyme they hung the flowers one at a time on the hooks. Or you could buy self-adhesive hooks. Pound shops sell a card of thirty different sized hooks, and only a pound! We had completed a row of flowers. The garden was full.

Teaching tip: The flowers were very easily made by the children themselves. They painted a large flower and cut it out. The flowers were stuck onto a cereal box and usually cut round in exactly the same way as the child had cut, by an adult. If children are able to cut the card, then they should. A stalk was either painted at the same time as the flower or stuck on as a strip of paper afterwards. Instead of putting the flowers on the hooks, the child who had made it held it in front of them and they became part of the unnumbered number line. As flowers were 'picked' the child sat down with the rest of the group.

Back to the activity. What if we wanted to pick some of the flowers to put in a vase? No, not a vase, that wouldn't really be a clear enough image to show the flowers that had been collected. A row of vases would be better. An empty paint pot with wet sand at the bottom was the answer. We put together the same number of vases as we had flowers (1–1 correspondence), put the flowers in them and said the rhyme again, moving the vase flowers to the hooks.

After we had filled the garden I then looked at ways to 'pick' the flowers. What I wanted was to show the children the complete line of flowers and then, by picking them, see that the line becomes shorter, therefore illustrating that that there were fewer left. It is crucial at this point to make sure the picked flowers are taken from the right-hand end.

As the flowers were 'picked' they were placed in a vase, this time starting at the left end. We counted how many were still in the garden and then counted how many had been picked. This led to counting them all together. There were always six! And what interested the children was the fact that as one row of flowers got shorter, the other row got longer. Amazing!

I wondered what would happen if we took two flowers at a time. Would the same thing happen? Let's find out.

And we did. And it did. This was reaching excitement level. Let's take three flowers at a time. What a discovery. When we picked three flowers there were still three flowers left.

We then went on to pick four, five and six to discover what would happen. But, oh dear, four and five still left flowers in the garden. But six was a good one because all of the flowers went from the garden into the vases.

I wonder what the children will remember when they start looking at multiplication patterns. Maybe nothing, but we enjoyed the activity!

Letters on houses

Fired by the success of this 'number line' I was on a mission to find more hooks and different ways of using them. Instead, I found different hooks which could be used in a very similar way.

An ideal way to capture the interest and concentration of the children is by linking it to Postman Pat.

Buy from a pound shop a pack of envelopes. They can be the same colour or two different colours, which I'll tell you about later.

Hole-punch one end and thread some string through. The envelopes are now ready to hang on the door hooks.

Sing the Postman Pat song with the children so that they can add the actions of waving, knocking and ringing. If you're unsure of the words of the song, you can easily find them online.

From a charity shop I managed to find a postman's hat, but any good dressing-up or toy shop will have one. But mine cost just thirty pence!

One child wears the postman's hat and holds the letters. As the last line is sung, the postman delivers a letter. As before, start at the left side of the line (in this case the street). A different child can be the postman for each letter, or one can be the postman for all of the letters. It's up to you.

As the letters are being 'posted' talk about how many there are, how many are left, how many altogether and so on.

Using two different colours for your envelopes

I chose to use two colours, as we could look at the pattern as they were hung. This would eventually lead to odd and even numbers.

Working to five is an ideal way to start this activity but some children may be ready to work to ten or beyond. You have two options for ten. Either put two envelopes on each hook or buy another hook rack.

Link this with letter-writing. Write a letter to your friend or your family. It could be an invitation to a class event, a story or just a chatty one. Or write a letter to a favourite character from a book. Children can then hang their letters on the hooks.

Younger children may use their own language and their own way of writing but it leads into:

> **Writing:** Children use their phonic knowledge to write words in ways which match their spoken sounds. They also write some irregular common words. They write simple sentences which can be read by themselves and others. Some words are spelt correctly and others are phonetically plausible.
>
> (Statutory Framework for
> the Early Years Foundation Stage, DfE, March 2012)

Pegs

Some stories just lend themselves beautifully to the use of pegs as an early no-number number line.

Mrs Mopple's Washing Line *by Anita Hewett*

Poor Mrs Mopple. Hanging out the washing has been so much trouble, and when the wind blows, some very strange things happen. It starts with a pig in a petticoat, and things soon become even more amazing.

Walter's Windy Washing Line *by Neil Griffiths*

Walter had hoped to enjoy a Saturday morning watching his favourite television programmes while his mum went shopping. All seemed perfect, until an unexpected gust of wind spoilt his plans.

   I have managed to find different pegs that suit most stories but they are very easy to make. Buy a cheap pack of wooden pegs and stick pictures onto them. Job done.

   For Mrs Mopple's washing line, the base card is that of a washing line. We use a small box die with pictures to match the pegs stuck on each face. Children take turns to throw the die and collect their matching peg. Each peg has its own space on the line, which is marked in sections.

   The rule is that there cannot be more than one of each type of clothing. For some children this is the beginning of 'miss a turn' but, within the fun of the game, this sometimes gets overlooked by the child, or there could be a major meltdown. Either way, see it as an opportunity to develop social skills and living by rules.

   As time goes on you may want to add numbers to the sections. This will translate into a *number track* where the numbers (and pegs) are in between the marks where numbers would go on a *number line*. You will then be in a position where you can talk about how many, how many more.

Change what is on the box die to have one face with a windy symbol. This will mean that an item of clothing has blown off the line and needs to be removed. So talk about how many now, how many are left if one blows away.

Change the peg and change the activity.

Use pegs with bees on for any Winnie-the-Pooh story where bees are involved. On the box die use three faces of bees and three faces of honey jars.

If a honey jar is thrown, add a honey-jar peg to the number line or track. If a bee is thrown, take off a honey jar.

It is possible for some children to work to ten. In this case make five of the faces honey jars and only one face bees, or you may have a very long game! It's all about probability!

As before, only add the numbers when the children are ready and after a great deal of talking and discussing and sharing ideas.

Use animal or minibeast pegs

Link with any story with animals or minibeasts; for instance, *The Bad-Tempered Ladybird* by Eric Carle.

How many friends did the Bad-Tempered Ladybird invite to his party?

Use your box die and put one of each of the minibeasts on different faces of the box.

Prepare the empty number track or line as before. Children take turns to throw the die, collect that peg and peg it on. When the card is full, take all of the pegs off and sort them into like groups. Peg one group on one card, the second group on a different card and so on, until all of the pegs are pegged.

Compare the lengths of the lines of pegs to find the longest line. And what does that mean? It means the most. And the shortest line is the least. Was it the butterflies or the bees? The ladybirds or the caterpillars?

Change the pegs, change the story, but the activity stays the same. I look for children who show understanding of the concept whatever the situation. When they show that, it's time to move on.

Knitted socks

You can find a pattern for a knitted sock in the chapter on resources.

I remember well the hours I spent darning socks back in the old days. But now they have become part of the throwaway way of life.

Don't throw them away. Use them for puppets (wash them well first!). Or go to your local market or pound shop where you will be able to buy multiple packs for a very small amount of money.

When I started this idea I used white sports socks because I didn't want anything getting in the way of the children focussing on the numbers. But you may like to use brightly-coloured ones, stripy ones, spotty ones. Again, the choice is yours.

As it turned out, these first socks didn't have numerals but there was a lot of talk and discussion about 'how many' and 'we two can play together. We can have a puppet each' and 'we need another puppet for Ruby'. Who needs numbers when the talk was so rich and exciting, and helped on with open questions such as 'How do you know when you've got enough puppets for everyone?'

To start with children used the socks as straightforward puppets. The range of stories and situations that were invented with just a sock on the end of an arm was amazing. It's a bit like Lego and a toy car. The toy car will always be a toy car, but Lego can be anything you want it to be. Try using white socks – they can become anything you want them to be.

Over time we added eyes, hair and a tongue that flapped when the mouth was open. Another brilliant idea for imaginative play and storytelling by adults or children.

Once plenty of playing had been enjoyed, those puppets began to evolve into version two. These were hand-knitted ones. As with any new resource, give children plenty of playing time before asking them to use them in a more focussed way.

A band of willing volunteers from the local Women's Institute took up the challenge to produce ten puppets where no two were alike. And all it cost was a box of (luxury!) biscuits.

Needles were flying, news and gossip were exchanged. Seams were stitched and eyes were securely sewn on. It just needed the final touch of the numerals or spots. These started with spots in the dice/domino pattern up to five. But you can make up to three or ten depending on the children you are working with. I have to say that anything over five may need a bigger puppet. Trying to fit ten spots on was a challenge!

We then made up a monster rhyme, trying to find rhyming words that made sense.

One baby monster, alone and new.
Finds a friend, and now there are two.
Two baby monsters walk to the sea.
They find another, and now there are three.
Three baby monsters open the door.
They find another, and now there are four.
Four baby monsters go for a drive.
Along comes another and now there are five.

It started with the one-spot monster who stood alone (looking sad). The other monsters roared while opening the mouths of the puppets. One-spot monster had to find two-spot monster and they held hands. The other monsters closed the puppet mouths. When it got to three, the actions were repeated but this time two-spot monster had to find three-spot monster, but could have help from one-spot if it was needed. They all held hands. And so on until all five were holding hands.

The children loved joining in with the roaring! Be prepared for some sore throats.

The spots were replaced by numerals and eventually they went up to ten. Then there was the opportunity to look at number bonds to ten with the older children. Three monsters holding hands, how many more do we need to collect?

Make a flip book of 'Ten in the Bed', but have monsters instead of people.

Back to frogs: borders for a flower-bed

Other people queue outside large, well-known shops when there is a sale on. Not me! I wait until one of the pop-up pound shops is about to close and move on and I am there, the first customer of the day. On this day you can practically buy the whole shop for a pound! And look what I found.

There were five frogs in each pack and I bought four packs for a pound. Twenty frogs! They are designed to spike into your border edge (or round a pond) and link together to form a quaint yet quirky border.

A border? Whatever for? Because I can get four sets of 'five speckled frogs' for a pound.

This is what I did.

Each frog was stood in a bucket of wet sand, so that the spikes were well protected.

Teaching tip: Don't set them in concrete. It may prove to be too tempting for a child to pick up the frog and whirl the whole thing round his or her head. Remember the brick in a bag for the Three Little Pigs?

We counted five frogs into their buckets and began the rhyme. As each frog jumped into the pool, one of the frogs was removed. This continued until all of the frogs had 'jumped'. Five frogs in the buckets, five frogs out of the buckets. In, out, in, out, in, out. It was amazing how many times the children wanted to do this activity.

But time to move on.

Each frog then acquired a tummy. On this tummy was one, two, three, four or five bugs. As a class we counted the bugs. We talked about more than and less than. The frogs were then put in order, according to the number of bugs, starting with one and going in order to five. The bugs were drawn in the dice/domino pattern.

As with 'Ten in the Bed', we either removed number one frog first, linking 'one' and 'first', or we started at the other end so that the number of bugs on the next frog to be removed told us how many frogs were left.

Of course, the next stage was to put the numbers in place of the bugs. I stuck the bugs on one side of the tummy and the numbers on the other so they were quickly interchangeable.

Penguins

The end of December is a good time to look for unusual bargains that are greatly reduced and can be used in the classroom. These penguins originally held a small bag of sweets which I managed to eat!

As the penguins came with clips already attached, there was no need to do anything much to them.

We threaded them onto a broom handle and moved them along as they were counted.

At the back of each penguin was a small zip. One day I put a small toy car inside one of them. The children were asked to feel each penguin to try to find the one with a toy inside. Once it was found, it was hung on the handle. One penguin, one toy. But what should the next penguin have? If we hung it on the handle we would then have two penguins. If one penguin had one toy, how many toys do you think should be in number two penguin? (The answer is two for those of you who may have lost a bit of interest in penguins!) Out of a tray of small-world toys, two children were dispatched to find a toy each so that when they were together (the toys, not the children), both would fit in the penguin bag. That penguin was then hung next to the one already there so that we now had two penguins with one and two toys.

The third penguin was next and the whole activity was repeated. This time it was quite a challenge to find three small toys that fitted into the bag, but we managed! But I doubt if we could have made a whole line to ten.

The next stage was to make black felt numerals of 1, 2 and 3. Felt was used because it stuck onto the fur fabric of the penguins and could be easily removed.

As we counted the toys, the appropriate numeral was put on the tummy of the penguin. The penguins were hung on the broom handle and we counted along while I pointed to the numbers. We counted forwards and we counted backwards. We muddled the penguins up and counted again, but this time we reorganised them so that they were in the right numerical order.

The activity continued with some children counting the toys to help them while others used the numbers. Some children chose the number and then checked with the toys.

Calendars

Talking about the end of the year and looking forward to the beginning of the next one, look for calendars. Or, to be more precise, look for calendars round about July when they sell for fifty pence.

You will have a diary for the dates; you need the calendars for the pictures.

I gave my son a calendar one year as a present but had already cut the pictures from the bottom half. He was a little surprised! My comment was that he only needed the dates, so, rather than wait a year, I had the pictures. His comment? 'I wonder if you will ever give us presents where you don't want all or some of it back again!'

And what is the moral of this story? Choose gifts for family and friends carefully. You may need them back again!

There are many, many different pictures you can use, but look for ones with number content. It can be the same pictures, just more or fewer of them, or it can be different: cars, boats, trains – anything really.

You may want to go up to ten or just up to five. For some children, recognising one and more than one is a huge achievement.

Sort the pictures into groups of one and more than one. Progress to including two and more than two. Some children may be able to accomplish this much sooner than others. It may be 'one, two, lots' for some for quite a while.

Greeting cards

Greeting cards have been with us for many years. The ancient Chinese sent cards to celebrate their New Year and the early Egyptians used papyrus scrolls. Many parents, grandparents, carers, aunts and uncles, brothers and sisters have been sent cards made with love and a great deal of glue and glitter. I still have every card each of my children made for me and now also have a box of cards from my grandchildren. These are precious memories. But there are now thousands of ready-made designs just waiting to be used, filling shops all over the world. Cards range in size, shape, colours, themes; there's a card for every occasion.

Sometimes the pictures will show low amounts, sometimes they will show huge amounts. It's quite valuable to talk about 'lots' or 'how many do you think there are?' or 'do you think there's more than ten?' Or even 'how do you think we could find out how many there are?'

Look at the dice card. Using the pattern of the spots ask children to find five, or two, or any number up to six. Ask if they can find a different die with the same number of spots. For older children, how about finding two dice that have a total of three, or less than nine, or three dice that total ten? Or how many different ways are there to make five using just these dice? The questions can be changed according to the age, ability and experience of the children.

'Look at the sweets. Tell me about what you can see. How many round sweets, how many yellow sweets?' And so on. Ask the older children to make up some questions of their own.

'How about the cows? How could we count the cows?' If there are too many, photocopy the picture, perhaps enlarged onto A3 paper, and get rid of half or a quarter of the cows. Ask the children for ways rather than telling them how to do it. If they don't know, make a suggestion as in 'I wonder if we . . . Would that work? Shall we try it?'

Lots and lots. Oh my goodness, how many characters are on the card at the bottom of the picture? You can talk about rows and columns. Later in school children will be looking at arrays to use with multiplication, so this is a very early introduction to this, by just looking at and talking about the picture.

How about the card with friends in pairs? A lovely 'talking about' card. Talk about your friend. Talk about gifts. 'What would you give your friend? What would you like your friend to give you? Why do you think they are giving gifts?' Again, this is a good design to give the idea of an array. Three groups of two going across (row) and seven groups of two going down (column).

Or how about using much simpler designs?

It's time to start searching. Use new cards, used cards, sent cards, received cards, number cards. There are lots just waiting to be found!

Handy hints

A **number line** is just that – a straight line with numbers placed at even spaces along its length. It's not a ruler, so the space between the numbers doesn't matter, but the numbers included on the line determine how it's meant to be used.

Number lines can be used throughout a child's time at primary school, starting in the early years; ordering numbers is an important skill and children can be given a blank number line and asked to put a variety of numbers in order on it.

Tips for parents and carers

If you create number lines for your children to help them at home, add colours, shapes or favourite characters to make them a little more interesting.

Make 3D number lines with small boxes. Turn the boxes inside out and paint them. Include your children in this. They love to paint! When the paint is dry, make one of them the head of a dragon, snake, worm or caterpillar and write numbers on the other sections. The animal can then be put together with the numbers in order, or only even numbers, or only odd numbers. You can make it as long as you like. Link it with a game. For instance, two players take turns to throw a 1–6 die. Each player collects a matching segment. Who can complete their line first?

You could add a Velcro circle to each end of the boxes so that they join together. Take out one box. Can your child tell you which number is missing? Or put them together in the wrong order. Ask your child to reorder them.

Look for number lines around your house. For example: a calendar, a clock, a tape measure.

Hide numbers within a room or the whole house. As they are found, ask your child to put them in order.

Put a set of numbers on the floor or a table. Ask 'Can you find me a number more than three, less than five?' and so on. As the numbers are chosen, place them on an empty number line in order.

Use a pack of cards with the pictures taken out. Cards have the added advantage of having the numbers represented by the symbols.

Chapter 5: Don't throw this away

This chapter looks at how to use all of those bits and pieces that you generally throw away – the piece of wool that is too short to make anything useful, or lids of coffee jars or jam jars. Many have been mentioned already throughout this book: bags, boxes and cardboard tubes; paperware such as plates, wrapping paper and serviettes; hair-related items such as hair bands and shower caps; and materials related to number lines.

Below are the learning objectives that I have specifically covered throughout this book.

Communication and language

Understanding: Children follow instructions involving several ideas or actions. They answer 'how' and 'why' questions about their experiences and in response to stories or events.

Listening and attention: Children listen attentively to stories.

Children listen attentively in a range of situations. They listen to stories, accurately anticipating key events, and respond to what they hear with relevant comments, questions or actions.

Speaking: Children develop their own narratives and explanations by connecting idea or events.

Children express themselves effectively, showing awareness of listeners' needs. They use past, present and future forms accurately when talking about events that have happened or are to happen in the future. They develop their own narratives and explanations by connecting ideas or events.

Reading: Children read and understand simple words.

Development: Involves giving children opportunities to experience a rich language environment; to develop their confidence and skills in expressing themselves; and to speak and listen in a range of situations.

Mathematics

Develop and improve children's skills in counting, understanding and using numbers; calculating simple addition and subtraction problems. Children investigate and experience things and 'have a go'.

Active learning: Children concentrate and keep on trying if they encounter difficulties and enjoy achievements.

Creating and thinking critically: Children have and develop their own ideas, make links between ideas and develop strategies for doing things.

Shape, space and measures: Children use everyday language to talk about weight, size, capacity, position and distance to compare quantities and objects and to solve problems.

Children use everyday language to talk about position and to solve problems. They explore characteristics of everyday objects and shapes and use mathematical language to describe them.

Numbers: Involves providing children with opportunities to develop and improve their skills in counting, understanding and using numbers, and calculating simple addition and subtraction problems.

Children count reliably with numbers from one to twenty, place them in order and say which number is one more or one less than a given number.

Using quantities and objects, they add and subtract two single-digit numbers.

An early years classroom is typically organised to promote the social skills and develop understanding of young children through stories, songs, rhymes, finger games and board games. The key ingredients are to give greater emphasis to children's developing language and to encourage all children to learn by working together.

There is no good reason why children with physical or sensory disabilities should always work on any sort of separate programme. For most of them it is simply a question of access, and materials should be adapted to meet their particular needs so that they can work alongside their peers.

So how does this match with the title of this chapter?

We seem to be a nation of 'throwaways' but there is a great deal of play value in things we don't need any more. These can be used as playing pieces for games.

Let's recap on some of the ideas shared with you throughout this book.

For a lot of children there is nothing so boring as a cube or a counter. You have green today and then blue tomorrow. Then you've peaked! You don't like any of the other colours. Let's see what we can do to interest a child in a game.

Firstly, the theme of a game needs to be suitable for the child who is playing it. This is where wrapping paper can play a huge part. Look in any stationer's shop and see what is currently engaging children. Once it stops being on wrapping paper then children may have moved on to the next craze/character/story. Dinosaurs are always popular but dragons are creeping up to join them. Robots and toys never go out of fashion. But there is also a huge collection that links with stories, television programmes or films.

Or use serviettes for simple games. These can be for matching, counting or following a route.

HINT: Don't use used ones. They are a bit tricky to get flat and clean. Use what's left in the packet.

Follow the way the turtles are walking to get the pattern of track games such as Snakes and Ladders. Put numbers in the cherries and throw a die to find a matching number. Cover the cherry with a red counter. For children counting to five use the penguins. Use a box die with the same pictures and a green face for 'have another turn'. Match the penguins in order.

Secondly, look at the playing pieces that can be used. Some children may need something larger than a counter. Use a coffee-jar lid instead, or the top of a fabric-softener bottle.

Or used party poppers, an empty shampoo bottle (glue the lid firmly on) or empty sweet containers.

Or use free items that you get from restaurants or fast-food outlets.

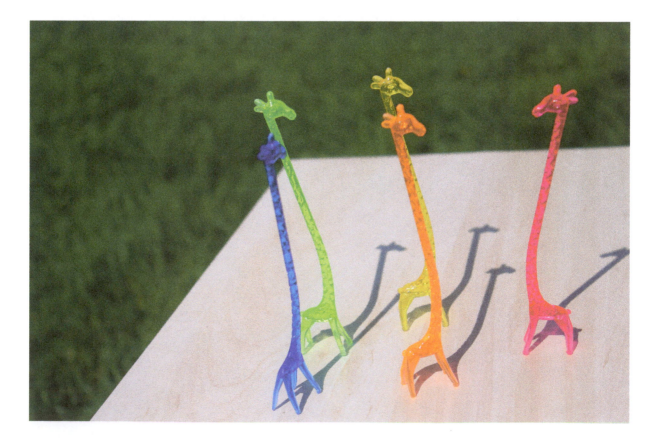

Thirdly, look at the dice that are being used. Some are too small to be handled safely, or the spots to be counted are too small. If this is the case, use a tissue box instead. Make your own cube from card.

Make a game for 'conservation' or 'bug life' or 'what's in the garden'. These pictures were cut from wrapping paper. Put them on the face of a tissue-box die and collect a matching bug each throw. Have ten throws each. Who has the most bees, caterpillars and so on? Use one-to-one correspondence to match the players' pictures. The longest line means the most. You don't have to count! Just look for the longest line.

Fourthly, have a huge range of resources so that children have a choice about which to use.

Games

Resources for games

Dice

Have as large a selection of different dice as possible. For example:

- Opaque, pearl, glitter, marble, clear
- 1–6 spot dice – various sizes, foam, plastic
- 7–12 number dice, 7–12 spot dice
- Dice using words instead of spots or numerals
- Blank – various sizes with round- and square-cornered form
- Shapes on each face
- Smiley face (have another turn), sad face (miss a turn)
- Colour dice with one colour per face. These can be found in charity or toy shops. Or, make your own!

Playing cards

Use playing cards such as:

- Picture cards
- Four-suits pack
- Blank playing cards – different sizes cut from card or the inside of a cereal box
- Shape cards; money cards; direction cards; colours.

Playing pieces

Think about playing pieces that will interest such as:

- Various sizes, textures and thicknesses
- Different colours
- Stand-up counters
- Stackable playing pieces.

Paper

Share a variety of papers so that children can make their own games.

- A4, A3, A2, A1 in assorted colours for baseboards or for cutting and sticking onto the board
- Sticky paper shapes – assorted sizes
- Stickers.

'But what about storage?' I hear you ask. Well . . .

- Plastic containers for dice. These can be small, washed-out margarine tubs or larger ice-cream boxes.
- Colour-coded zip wallets to store games – A4 and A3 and black-handled wallets A3, A2, A1 to store larger games. And a wooden coat rack to hang them on. If you have a covered area these can be on the wall outside the classroom but they should be accessible for children to be able to choose a game.

Use labels to write the contents of the wallet; this helps at 'tidy up time'. And find large plastic stackable boxes – with lids if possible.

Children love to play games, whether at home, in the street, in the park, in the playground or in the classroom. What better way is there to introduce and reinforce concepts than to make learning fun through games?

For children who have difficulties with learning, where confidence may have hit rock bottom, the security of repetitive exercises in a workbook can be replaced by active participation generated by playing games pitched at an appropriate level of challenge.

Interpreting, discussing, following rules, making decisions and asking questions all lead to generating positive attitudes towards learning.

Playing games allows children to:

- Use and extend their vocabulary
- Learn about cooperation and support of each other

- Build confidence
- Foster home–school relationships when the games are used at home.

Games are an excellent resource for motivating and encouraging children to become involved in a mathematical activity. They take away the 'fear' of mathematics. They are unthreatening. Many children, in fact, don't realise that they are 'doing' maths. Comments such as 'but we haven't done our maths today' are common! A positive spin-off is that parent-helpers in school are often much happier playing a game or solving a puzzle with a group of children than they would be if asked to 'do some maths'. As long as the teacher explains the mathematical purpose behind the game (this can easily be put as part of the rules), suggests appropriate vocabulary and perhaps questions to ask, most parents are confident enough to have a go.

Encourage children to take a game home to play. If you start a games library in the school, remember that out-of-class activities need to be frequent, short and focussed. They should be varied, interesting and fun, so that they motivate children, stimulate their learning and foster different learning skills.

Ask for comments from someone at home who has played the game with the child. Maybe ask for suggestions for new games. Then ask them into school to help make them!

Games can build confidence for children across the ability range. Games of chance are particularly good for this as all children, regardless of ability, have an equal chance of winning. For these games, the groupings can be similar ability, friendship groups, mixed ability or any other grouping that the teacher or child wants to introduce.

And last but not least, games act as an incentive to improve existing skills and reinforce new skills.

Games can:

- Allow children to explore and discuss ideas.
- Allow children to develop appropriate vocabulary. Write a list of the words that you want the children to use, or incorporate them into the game itself.
- Link learning with enjoyment in a very practical way. We all learn best when we enjoy what we are doing.
- Encourage children to interact socially and develop their communication skills by allowing children to talk together, discussing rules, looking at strategies for winning, or working out where there was a wrong move.
- Encourage children to work cooperatively.
- Promote increased concentration.
- Help children to memorise facts.

It is very important to plan the games carefully, and to be clear about why you are using them. Although children will have a favourite game that they will like to play most of the time, it is important to introduce new games or extensions of favourites at regular intervals. They can be introduced gradually, making sure that the children understand what the game is about and how they play it.

I have found it better not to give long detailed instructions when introducing a new game. Keep it short and simple. Make the rules clear, with no ambiguity. You can bet that if there are two ways of interpreting the rules, children will find them! This can lead to dispute and disruption. When you call a group together to play a game, get started straight away; don't waste time, or you'll lose the impact that you want to make.

If there needs to be a central character for the game, make sure that each player, at some point, gets to play the main part. This ensures that all players participate and that shy or less confident children are not dominated by more forceful personalities!

Involve all children in the group as soon as possible. Don't make the groups too large or children will get bored waiting for their turn.

Most important! If a game is failing, don't be afraid to stop it and start another one. Make the games fun. Don't make unnecessary rules. Don't stop the game to nag. Deal with individual disruption without the game being spoilt for the other players.

When planning a new game it is important to involve the children in making decisions. The more they are involved the more they will want to play, and the more practice they will have.

It is important to let the children know the purpose of the game they are playing.

And really, really important is to allow children time to develop games of their own.

I have found some rules help me when thinking of new games. For younger children, try to develop games around stories or rhymes that the children are familiar with. Make the theme of the games for all children interesting and appropriate. When designing the game, make the board bright and cheerful. Most children love colour. Look at the size of the board. Is it suitable for the age and ability of the children who will be playing? If the board is too small, the players will be squashed and the pieces will get knocked over. Or it may limit the number of children who can play the game. The board must be of a manageable size for the place where it is to be played. Use the floor for large games.

Make the playing pieces interesting. Cubes or counters can become boring. Match the playing pieces to the theme of the game. Free gifts from cereal packets are a good source. Another alternative is to use flour and salt dough. This can be made by the children, (involving them in work on ratio and proportion) and then used to make playing pieces.

For Snakes and Ladders, make long snakes, short snakes, straight snakes, curly snakes, wide snakes, narrow snakes, fat snakes and thin snakes. The beauty of having detachable playing pieces is that the game can be different every time it's played. Put on lots of ladders and one snake and you get to the end quickly. Put on lots of snakes and one ladder and the game can go on for hours! But the important thing is that each player has a turn to choose the pieces and place them on the board.

Have a clear purpose for the game, and have it clearly showing as part of the rules.

Limit the playing time. A game that goes on and on does little to keep the interest of the players. It's better to play the same game twice than to lose some of the players!

As I finish this part of the chapter on games and their benefits, here are some tips for making games for your setting. Clear instructions and simple rules, irrespective of reading levels, are essential. Some games may be taken home. Children may play with other members of the family. In the interest of family harmony, keep rules simple. Make the game appropriate for a mixed-age or mixed-ability audience. Include in the rules ideas for simplification and extension activities to keep older members of the family interested. Make the games fun. Make the game motivational so that the children want to play it again and again.

Remember that a game is only worth playing if it is right for the children who are playing it.

So far this book has offered tried-and-tested ideas to stimulate children and to provide ideas of free, cheap and recycled resources to inspire the learner and you, the teacher.

This chapter is asking you not to throw anything away as, eventually, it will be just what you need. Unfortunately, you may then live in a house like mine where two attics, a summerhouse, a garage and a study (and usually handy floor space) are filled with 'this will be useful one day' junk!

As I approach my next decade it is finally time to sort and clear. But stop! What is this that I have found?

Scraps of knitting wool

No more sorting and clearing for me. This is exactly what I wanted for my number puppets.

I can feel you itching to have a set of your own.

Here's how to make one. Just stitch a felt number inside the mouth.

You will need:

Odd balls of double knit wool in four or five colours. (This pattern assumes five colours.)

A pair of size 3.00 mm (UK size 11) needles

A stitch holder

Abbreviations:

K	knit
K2tog	knit the next two stitches together
P	purl
st(s)	stitch(es)
st st	stocking stitch (one row knit, one row purl)

How to increase by knitting into the same stitch twice:

Knit the next stitch as you normally would, but before dropping the stitch from the left needle, knit into the back of that stitch.

1st piece:

Using yarn A cast on 40 sts.

First row *K1 P1 * repeat from * to the end of the row.
Repeat the first row 5 more times.

Join yarn B. Work 6 rows in st st.
Join yarn C. Work 6 rows in st st.
Join yarn D. Work 6 rows in st st.
Join yarn E. Work 6 rows in st st.

Rejoin yarn A. Knit 20 sts, put remaining 20 sts on a stitch holder. Turn.
Purl 1 row.
Next row K2tog. Knit to last 2 stitches. K2tog.
Purl 1 row.
Repeat the last 2 rows 3 more times (12 sts remaining).
Next row K, increasing on the first and last sts.
Purl 1 row.
Repeat the last 2 rows 3 more times (20 sts).
Knit 1 row.
Purl 1 row.

Rejoin yarn C. Work 24 rows in st st.
Cast off knitwise.

Pick up 20 stitches from the stitch holder.
Work 24 rows in st st.
Cast off knitwise.

2nd piece:

Cast on 20 stitches in yarn C.

Work 24 rows in st. st.

Cast off.

To make up:

Stitch decreased edges of yarn A, right side to right side.

Stitch side edges of striped section right side to right side.

Stitch cast-on edge of 2nd piece to cast-off edge of 1st side of 1st piece.

Stitch cast-off edge of 2nd piece to cast-off edge of 2nd side of 1st piece.

Decorate with facial features (eyes, tongue) to right side of work before stitching side edges together.

It's not as difficult as it seems! And well worth it.

And finally, never ever throw away empty tins that were once filled with biscuits. Many shops now sell 'themed' tins. These are wonderful when planning a 'giant' day.

Chapter 6: Useful resources

This last chapter adds some meat to the bones of previous ideas and summarises some important points.

Provide stimulating resources which are accessible and open-ended so they can be used, moved and combined in a variety of ways. Make sure resources are relevant to children's interests and plan first-hand experiences and challenges appropriate to the development of the children.

We want children to be involved and concentrating, maintaining focus on their activity for a period of time. I really love to see high levels of energy and fascination.

Children will become more deeply involved when you provide something that is new and unusual for them to explore, especially when it is linked to their interests. It is important to make sure that they have time and freedom to become involved in activities. Help children to keep ideas in mind by talking over photographs of their previous activities. Don't be too quick to have 'tidy up time'.

By allowing children to think and have their own ideas we are encouraging them to find ways to solve problems as well as finding new ways to do things. Sometimes we need to show them how a thinker evolves. Show that you don't always know, are curious and sometimes puzzled, and can think and find out. Always respect children's efforts and ideas, so they feel safe to take a risk with a new idea. Give children time to talk and think.

Model the creative process, showing your thinking about some of the many possible ways forward. Sustained, shared thinking helps children to explore ideas and make links. Follow children's lead in conversation, and think about things together. Encourage children to describe any problems they have and suggest ways to solve the problem.

Play is a key opportunity for children to think creatively and flexibly, solve problems and link ideas. Play allows children to use their creativity while developing their imagination, dexterity, and physical, cognitive and emotional strength. Play is important to healthy brain development. It is through play that children at a very early age engage and interact with the world around them.

Play is what children and young people do when they follow their own ideas and interests, in their own way, and for their own reasons.

Play has also frequently been described as 'what children and young people do when they are not being told what to do by adults'.

Playing is one of the most important things parents can do with their children. The time spent playing together gives children lots of different ways and times to learn.

Play helps a child:

- Build confidence
- Feel loved, happy and safe
- Develop social skills, language and communication
- Learn about caring for others and the environment
- Develop physical skills.

There are many benefits of using games. The advantages have been summarised in an article by Davies (1995):

- Meaningful situations – for the application of skills are created by games.
- Motivation – children freely choose to participate and enjoy playing.
- Positive attitude – games provide opportunities for building self-concept and developing positive attitudes through reducing the fear of failure and error.
- Increased learning – in comparison to more formal activities, greater learning can occur through games due to the increased interaction between children and problem solving strategies.
- Different levels – games can allow children to operate at different levels of thinking and to learn from each other. In a group of children playing a game, one child might be encountering a concept for the first time, another may be developing his/her understanding of the concept, a third consolidating previously learnt concepts.
- Assessment – children's thinking often becomes apparent through the actions and decisions they make during a game, so the teacher has the opportunity to carry out diagnosis and assessment of learning in a non-threatening situation.
- Home and school – games provide 'hands-on' interactive tasks for both school and home.
- Independence – children can work independently of the teacher. The rules of the game and the children's motivation usually keep them on task.

Making and playing games with children are two of the things I love most. There are many different types of games that can be developed:

- Races
- Board games
- Spatial strategy games
- Numerical strategy games
- Card games
- Matching games
- Mystery games.

Over the years there has been a lot of research done by well-respected educators. Below are just a few sources. A search on the internet will give you many, many more.

> Games provide an opportunity to fire children's enthusiasm.
>
> Fryer, 1996

> Taking turns when playing games and interacting with others will help to develop the children's social skills.
>
> QCA, 2000

> There are important implications for using talk for assessment purposes; children often know more than their written secretarial or transcription skills may reveal.
>
> Reynolds, 1996

Game boards

Here are just a few ideas for game boards that I have used with very young children. Change, add to or adapt for children you work with. Put them on paper, on a brick wall with chalk, paint them on the playground. Anywhere will do. Just get children playing!

Game board 1 – Straight track with pathways

Aims:

To follow rules

To count on in ones

To relate numerals to quantity.

This game can be played at different levels according to the age and ability of the players. Each player has one, two, three or four counters. This will depend on how long the game is to last. The counters are placed on Start and each player takes turns to throw a die and move one of their counters that number of spaces.

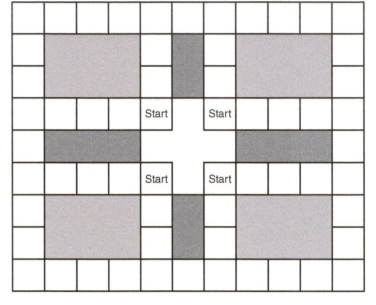

Handy hints

- Use as reinforcement for colour-matching, where each player has the same colour counter as the spaces they move on.
- If only small rectangles are being used, don't colour the rest of the board, as this may be confusing for younger players.

Ideas for games

At the most basic level, players will move their counters only round the rectangle that is joined to their start position. The rectangles can be coloured the same as a set of counters, each rectangle being a different colour. When a player reaches the start again, that counter is placed in the central reservation. Play continues until all of the counters have reached 'Home'.

Play begins as before but players move from Start in any direction round the outside edge of the board until they reach their Start again. As before, the counters are then placed in the central reservation.

Colour some of the squares the same as the counter colours. When a player lands on a square and the colour is the same, they can have another turn. If the colour is not the same, they miss a turn.

As above, but if a player lands on a colour that is not the same as their counter they must return to the start. HINT: This version only works with children who have patience and perseverance!

Game board 2 – Hexagon

Aims:

Simple matching

To make decisions

To develop strategies.

This is a game for up to four players. Each player takes turns to
throw a die and match what is on
the die to the same colour/object/
picture on the board.

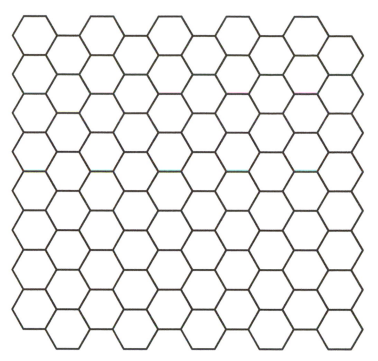

Handy hints

- The board can be made larger
  or smaller according to the age
  and ability of the players.
- Use pictures of characters that are well known to the children. Put matching pictures
  on a large blank die.
- Colour some or all of the sections, or stick on gummed paper shapes, and put matching colours on a blank die.
- After laminating the board, use PVA glue, which can be easily removed afterwards,
  to stick tactile samples on, and match them on a large die.
- Numbers can be written so that the board can be used as a number match, or use
  spots on the die so that players count the spots and find the matching numeral.
- Use dice or domino spot patterns as well as random spots on the board, and use a
  number die to match.
- For older or more able children ask them to cover three or four in a row, using their
  own colour counters. The three or four can be in any direction. Older children may
  begin to use strategies to block their opponents.

Ideas for games

The pictures used on this game board really have no relevance to the game other than
to catch the children's interest. Because of this, many games can be made with different
themes, which will allow the children to match, make decisions and develop strategies
without becoming bored with the context.

Link with any stories or number rhymes that have a connection with bees. This will
work well with the hexagonal cells. Players throw a die and move that number of places
across the game board. The first player to get across is the winner. However, fill some
of the spaces with pictures of bees; if a player lands on a bee they miss a turn. Fill some
of the spaces with pictures of honey jars and if a player lands on these spaces they have
another turn.

Fill the spaces with characters from a book or television programme that the children
know well and make a matching die or spinner. As the children throw the die or spin the
spinner they match and cover a picture on the game board. The first player to place five

or ten counters on the board is the winner. If an opponent throws or spins a character where all cells containing that character have been covered, an opponent's counter can be removed and given back to the player.

Players can develop strategies to block other players when trying to make three or four in a row.

Game board 3 – Stories/nursery rhyme board

Aims:

Putting maths into a relevant context

Counting along a track

Recognising numerals and relating them to quantity

Making decisions.

This game board can represent any favourite story or nursery rhyme. There are two start positions for either two or four players. If four players, they use the same playing piece and take turns to throw the die and move along the track.

Where the track crosses over, players must choose which path to follow.

Handy hints

- Illustrate the board, making it fit a story or rhyme. For example: take out the cottage and add a castle for Jack and the Beanstalk; add more trees to make a forest for Sleeping Beauty; put in flowers and a woodcutter for Red Riding Hood.
- Add numbers so that children count along the track, using the numerals as a prompt. In this case there will be no decisions to be made at a crossroads, as the players will follow the numbers in order.
- Colour some of the sections to make obstacles: tired, miss a turn; fall in the pond, miss a turn; have a drink and move on two spaces.
- Colour some sections for 'have another turn' or 'miss a turn'.
- Colour some sections so that when a player lands on a coloured one, they pick a card from a face-down pile. Each card in the pile has a character, cut from a comic or a sheet of wrapping paper, related to the theme of the game. If a player collects two characters the same, they miss a turn and return the last card picked up to the bottom of the pile.

Ideas for games

Use each enclosure as a field for Old MacDonald's animals. The players can collect animals as they move along the track. The animals can be pictures on cards. Each player must collect one of each before they can return to the farmhouse. This will involve children using strategies to plan their route. Change the number of animals so that players are involved in counting larger quantities.

Have two players, one as Red Riding Hood and the other as the Wolf. Who will get to Grandmother's cottage first? Will Grandma be safe with Red Riding Hood or eaten by the Wolf?

Use for Hansel and Gretel as they find their way through the forest. The house can become the gingerbread cottage or their own home. Add some spooky characters along the way!

Game board 4 – Curved track with pathways

Aims:

To recognise numbers

To count forwards in ones

To relate numbers with quantity.

Each player has a different starting space, and will count along the track according to the number showing on the die. The first player to reach the finish is the winner.

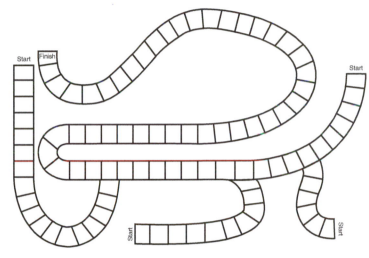

Handy hints

- Talk with the children about possible themes for the game. Children could have their own copy to illustrate.
- If the spaces are too small for some children in the class, take out some of the lines. Remember to keep the game fair, by ensuring that each player, wherever they start, has to move the same number of spaces as the other players to reach the end.
- Add rules by colouring some of the spaces: have another go; miss a turn; move on one space; move back one space. Each colour represents a rule.

Ideas for games

This board game is ideal for any 'journey' games and can be easily linked with stories. For example, as a game for four players, use the story of the Three Little Pigs with the wolf, or the Three Billy Goats Gruff with the troll, or even Cinderella with two ugly sisters and a prince! Each player places a counter on their own start and, throwing a die, moves that number of spaces. An appropriate picture can be drawn at the finish: a house for the pigs, a field for the goats, and a castle for Cinderella. As play continues, rules can be added: If the wolf lands on the same space as a pig, the pig must return to the start; the troll does the same to the goats and the two sisters do the same to Cinderella. If the prince and Cinderella land on the same space as each other, they move two places nearer the castle. If Cinderella or the prince land on a space already occupied by an ugly sister, they send that sister back to the start. Who will be the first to get to the castle and, therefore, marry the prince?

Add illustrations to make the game board into a moon landscape, where the players become astronauts. Who will get to the spaceship (finish) first?

Make the players into aliens who are racing to the spaceship to capture it.

Have two players as aliens and two as spacemen. Who will manage to escape from the planet before an alien takes over the ship?

Game board 5 – A 5 × 5 grid with spinner

Aims:

Matching

Counting

Comparing.

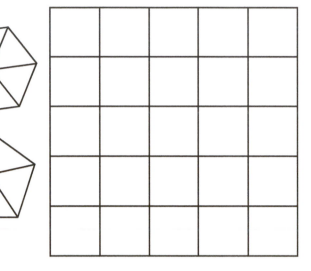

For younger or less able children cut the grid size down to 3 × 3. There needs to be an odd number of squares on the grid, so that, at the end of the game there is a winner. This is essential when comparing quantities, more than and less than. If you also want to look at 'the same as', use a 2 × 2 or 4 × 4 grid.

Handy hints

- Choose five or six pictures to fill the grid randomly, reproducing them in either the pentagon or hexagon you are using. Place a large paper clip in the middle of the shape, holding it in place with the point of a pencil. Players take turns to spin the clip and cover a matching picture on the grid. Sometimes a player will have to miss a turn, if all the pictures that match have been covered.
- Players have their own coloured interlocking cube. When the grid is full, players takes their own colour from the board and link them together. The player with the tallest tower or longest 'snake' of cubes is the winner.
- Use pictures that will interest the children: cartoon or story figures; characters from favourite television shows; cut-out pictures from comics or wrapping paper.

Ideas for games

This is an ideal way to produce a lot of games that have the same rules but which look different to the children. The cells in the grid can have favourite television characters, characters from books or any seasonal theme. By changing the pictures, the game will look different to the children, but replaying it will reinforce matching at its simplest level. It is also ideal for older children working at lower levels, as the illustrations can be age-appropriate.

Send a copy of the blank grid home with the children and ask them to make a game at home. This can be 'homework'. Children can then bring their games back to school and share them with the rest of the class or group.

Game board 6 – A 5 × 5 grid with 3 × 2 grid

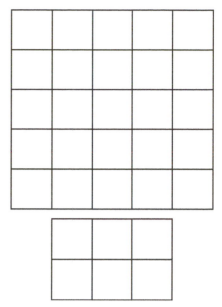

Aims:

Matching

Counting

Comparing

Number recognition.

This board is based on the previous one, but is an extension of it. This version has the characters placed in the smaller grid below the main one. As a space in the smaller grid is filled, write a number 1–6 next to it. Each player takes turns to throw a 1–6 die, match the number to the number on the grid, match that number to the picture next to it, and then match that picture to a picture in the larger grid. Play then continues as before, with players placing their own coloured interlocking cube on the space.

Handy hints

- Don't always use 1–6 dice. Make the dice fit the mathematical objectives and ability of the children playing the game: 1, 2, 3, 1, 2, 3; shape; money; spots; numerals, etc.
- Include the children in making decisions about the characters to place in the grid. If they're interested in them, they're more likely to play.

Ideas for games

Once the children are familiar with the rules, change them! In the grid write 2, 3, 4, 5, 6, 7 and use a 1–6 die. The rules: throw the die, add one, find the new number, match the number to the picture, picture to picture, and cover.

Change the rules again to: whatever you throw, double it. Change the numbers in the grid to match the rule.

Change the rules so that the players will be practising tables facts: whatever you throw, multiply by five, ten, three, seven, and so on. Write the appropriate numbers in the bottom grid.

Game board 7 – Simple straight track

Aims:

To encourage counting round a track

To encourage recognition of numbers

To reinforce number bonds to ten.

A square track such as this one can be used in a variety of ways, according to the interest and ability of the players. As each side has ten sections, using number bonds to ten or counting in tens can develop from that.

Handy hints

- Before laminating the board, colour some of the squares along each side, so that each side has its own colour. The corner squares should be divided diagonally so that the colour nearer to a side is the same as the side it touches. These coloured sections can be randomly placed or equally spaced. Each player chooses a coloured counter that corresponds to one of the colours on the board – with each player having a unique colour. As children count round the board, and land on a colour the same as their own, they have another turn. If they land on a colour not their own, they miss a turn. Younger or less able players can ignore the colours if they are not appropriate.
- Use various ideas from wrapping paper to interest the children.

Ideas for games

If using the board for reinforcing number bonds to ten, number the sections 1–10 along each side. As the child moves along ask questions such as 'How many places have you moved? How many more do you need to move before you go to a different colour?'

Number the board so that the number the child lands on also has the bond to make it to ten. These can be colour coded. Use a 1–10 die.

Fill the squares with numbers, coins, coin stamps or stickers, shapes, colours and so on, so that the game will reinforce the mathematical objectives of a lesson.

Add illustrations or decorations to the board to make it attractive and to fit with the theme: shopping pictures for a money game, for instance.

Each player chooses one side which will be their track. Draw a green bottle in each section, two in each corner section. Players take turns to throw a die and move that number of spaces either forwards or backwards along their own track. As they land on a 'bottle' they collect a green counter from a central pile. On their next turn they can choose to move forwards or backwards according to the number thrown. If they land on another green bottle they collect another green counter. If they move into an opponent's space by turning a corner, they miss a turn and go back to where they were. The first player to collect ten green bottles is the winner.

VARIATION: Cover each section with a green counter. As a player lands on one of their own sections they collect the green counter. Once a counter has been removed, it cannot be replaced. If a player lands on an empty section, they miss a turn. As before the player who collects all ten 'bottles' first is the winner. Be flexible with the rules. Allow a player to move in both directions in one turn if necessary. This may avoid frustration!

Draw a treasure island in the space inside the circuit and make a treasure game. The children can be pirates or treasure-hunters. For young children let them wear hats (to be pirates or sailors) and perhaps an eye patch. Place items of treasure, or draw them, on the spaces of the track. Make a matching pack of cards with the same drawings. As children land on some treasure, they either collect and keep it or collect a card with the treasure drawn on it. The winner is the player with most treasure. For older children make each item of treasure worth a certain amount. In this case, they total the value of their treasure and the player with the highest total is the winner. Add some obstacles that mean that treasure has to be returned or given to another player.

Game board 8 – Simple curved track

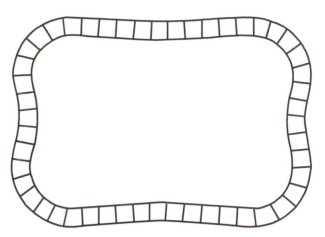

Aims:

To encourage counting round a track, backwards and forwards

To encourage recognition of numbers

To relate numerals to quantity.

The advantage of a track such as this one is that it is completely open, allowing the teacher to make it cover any aspect of mathematics. There is no conventional start or finish. Players choose where to start and that place will also be where they finish. They can also go round the track in either direction – but the direction they start in is the direction in which they continue, and they go round as many times as the game allows.

Handy hints

- Before laminating the board, decorate it with pictures from comics, which will attract the children to the game. Set the context of the game to suit the players' interests. Or illustrate it to fit in with a school or class theme.
- For younger or less able children, place a small sticker where they start, so that it is a clue for where their finish will be. If you want the player to go round the board more than once, place that number of stickers at the start, so that they can be peeled off one by one as the player passes.
- If there are too many sections, photocopy the board and remove every other line.
- Don't use only numbers in the sections: sometimes use coins, coin stamps or stickers, money values, shapes, colours and so on, depending on the mathematical theme of the lesson.
- Use different dice: number 1–6; spot 1–6; 1, 2, 3, 1, 2, 3 numerals; 1, 2, 3, 1, 2, 3 spots.

Ideas for games

Using any fairy story, decorate the board with the appropriate characters.

Colour some of the sections to match with the characters involved. For example, for Goldilocks and the Three Bears, randomly colour three or four sections yellow and the same amount brown. If the player taking the part of Goldilocks lands on a yellow section, they can have another go, but if they land on a brown section, they miss a turn. Similar rules apply for the 'bears': the brown sections mean have another turn, the yellow mean miss a turn.

Use the theme of 'racing' and use illustrations to show a race track. This can be cars, bikes or with a story or rhyme theme of 'The Hare and the Tortoise'. Introduce stopping areas, either as pit stops or animal resting places.

Useful recipes

These recipes can be used by parents, carers, teachers, helpers and children (given adequate supervision) to allow children to make and enjoy a whole range of items. Maybe pieces for a game board, maybe for a playing piece or maybe just because they can!

Basic dough

You will need:

    2 cups plain flour
    1 cup salt
    1 cup water
    1 tablespoon of cooking oil
    1 cup of powder paint or a good squeeze of ready-mixed paint
    A mixing bowl and spoon
    And, most important, an apron for anyone who is near to the mixing bowl.

1. Mix the dry ingredients together in the bowl.
2. Add the water and cooking oil (and ready-mixed paint, if using) and stir together.
3. Knead the dough to make it smooth.

Stretchy dough

Use the recipe for basic dough but replace the plain flour with self-raising flour. This will make puffy, stretchy dough with a very short life!

Long-lasting dough

This dough is very pliable and will keep for several months in an airtight container in a fridge.
    You will need:

    2 teaspoons cream of tartar
    1 cup plain flour
    Half a cup of salt
    1 tablespoon of cooking oil
    1 cup water
    A mixing bowl and spoon
    And the required aprons.

1. Mix all the ingredients together to form a smooth paste.
2. Put the mixture into a saucepan and cook slowly until the dough comes away from the sides of the pan and forms a ball.
3. Leave the dough to cool then remove it from the pan, add colouring if required and knead the dough for three to four minutes.
4. Soak the pan immediately.

Basic biscuits

You will need:

    125g (4oz) soft margarine or butter
    125g (4oz) sugar
    250g (8oz) plain flour
    1 egg
    A pinch of salt
    Bowl and spoon
    Rolling pin.

1. Beat the margarine and sugar together.
2. Beat the egg and add this to the mixture.
3. Sift in the flour and salt.
4. Mix to form a ball of dough.
5. Roll out and cut into shapes.
6. Bake on a greased tray in a moderate oven (190°C or Gas Mark 5) for about fifteen minutes.

Have them as part of a game. For example, eat them when you land on a square with a biscuit. Or just eat them!

Boxes

Use lots of different shapes and colours of boxes for play and for storage.

Hats

Even the youngest children can make marks on a hat. And believe me, they love the glue!

I have always found it a privilege to work and play with young children. There is no greater honour than being asked to join in their games.

Thank you for making it to the end of this book. Although, if you are anything like me, I usually start at the end!

One final quote:

> What we are teaches the child far more than what we say, so we must be what we want our children to become.
>
> Pearce, 1996

References

Bearne, E. (1996). *Differentiation and Diversity in the Primary School*, London, Routledge

Davies, B. (1995). 'The role of games in mathematics', *Square One*, Vol. 5 No. 2

Fryer, M. (1996). *Creative Teaching and Learning*, London, Paul Chapman Publishing Ltd

Pearce, J. C. (1996). Introduction. In: Childre, D. L. (1996). *Teaching Children to Love: 80 Games and Fun Activities for Raising Balanced Children in an Unbalanced World*, Boulder Creek, California, Planetary Publications

QCA (2000). *Curriculum Guidance for The Foundation Stage*, p. 48. London, QCA Publications

Mrs Mopple's Washing Line 57
My Cat Likes to Hide in Boxes 20

'Nine Hairy Monsters' 48–50
number bonds 60, 83–4
number lines 18, 35, 46–64; bags 31–2; developing
    a mental image 48; empty 47–8; flowers on hooks 53–5;
    frog beanbags 51–3; 'Incy Wincy Spider' 39; jumping
    frogs 60–1; knitted socks 58–60; letters on houses 55–6;
    moving animals along 40; 'Nine Hairy Monsters' 48–51;
    pastry and biscuit cutters 53; pegs 56–8; penguins 61–2;
    serviettes 9
number tracks 57–8
numbers 11, 19–20, 46, 66; game boards 78, 79, 80, 81,
    83; hair-related items 34, 35; 'Incy Wincy Spider' 39;
    paperware 3, 4, 5; sock puppets 59–60; 'Ten in the Bed' 28

'Old MacDonald Had a Farm' 4, 42–5
On the Farm game 32–3

paper 70
paper bags 14, 15–20, 31–2
paper plates 2–5
paperware 2–12
parents 11–12, 32, 45, 64
pastry cutters 53
peer group talk 11
pegs 56–8
penguins 61–2, 67
phonics 16, 56
pictograms 52, 53
picture cards 44–5
pictures: bugs 25; calendars 62; game boards
    79, 82, 85; greeting cards 63; kitchen rolls 10–11; '
    Nine Hairy Monsters' 49–51; paper plates 4;
    wrapping paper 6
pipe lagging 37–8
plastic bags 20
play 76
playing cards 64, 70
playing pieces 67–8, 70, 72
position 34
positive attitude 77
'Postman Pat' 56
problem solving 76
puppets 15–16, 40, 59, 73–5

quantity 19–20, 78, 80–1, 82

reading 13, 65
recipes 85–7
resources 69–72, 76–88
rhymes: 'Five Little Monkeys' 33; 'Five Little Speckled
    Frogs' 19–20, 51–3, 60–1; game boards 79, 80–1; games 72;
    grandchildren's 41–2; 'Incy Wincy Spider' 25, 36–9; 'Mary,
    Mary, Quite Contrary' 53; number lines 40, 48–9; 'Old

MacDonald Had a Farm' 4, 42–5; puppets 16; 'Ten in the
    Bed' 27–8, 60
role-play 16, 27
rubber stamps 6
rules 11, 12, 70, 71–2, 78, 83

scrunchies 35, 37, 40
self-esteem 43
serviettes 9–10, 66
shape 14, 22–3, 35, 66
shared thinking 76
shoe boxes 23, 27, 33
shower caps 41–5
Sleeping Beauty 16
snakes and ladders 7–9, 67, 72
snap 6, 9
social skills 44, 66, 71, 76, 77
socks 58–60
space 14, 35, 66
speaking 13, 16, 46, 65
stacking boxes 23–4
storage 70
stories 9, 13, 34, 72; bags 16–18, 30–1; game boards 79, 80–1,
    85; pegs 57
subtraction 33, 46

tablecloths 11
Teddy at the Seaside 9
'The Teddy Bears' Picnic' 26–7
'Ten in the Bed' 27–8, 60
'Three Little Pigs' 16–18
tins 75
toilet paper tubes 27
tracks 80, 81, 83–5; *see also* number tracks
treasure game 84
tubes 15, 27–30, 32, 37

'The Ugly Bug Ball' 25
understanding 65; bags, boxes and tubes 13; hair-related items
    34; number lines 46; paperware 2; wrapping paper 5

The Very Hungry Caterpillar 22–3
vocabulary: bags, boxes and tubes 14, 20; games 70, 71;
    hair-related items 34; number lines 47; paperware 3, 5

wallets 70
wallpaper 11
Walter's Windy Washing Line 57–8
weather 25, 38–9
weight 17–18
Winnie-the-Pooh 30, 58
wool 73–5
wrapping paper 5–9, 25, 26, 27, 66, 84
writing 16, 56

zoos 45

Index

active learning 5, 66
addition 46
animals: cardboard tubes 32; On the Farm game 32–3; game
    boards 80–1; number lines 40, 64; paper plates 4; paperware
    games 6, 7, 9; pegs 58; shower caps 41–5
arrays 63–4
Arthur's Dream Boat 9
assessment 77
attention 34, 65

The Bad-Tempered Ladybird 25, 58
bags 14, 15–20; On the Farm game 32–3; story
    bags 30–1
Beach 9
beanbags 51–3
bees 30, 58, 79
bingo 6–7, 10
binoculars 32
biscuit tins 75
biscuits 53, 86–7
boxes 14–15, 20–4, 32, 33, 87; box dice 24–7, 38–9, 43–4;
    number lines 64
bugs 19–20, 25–6, 69

calendars 62
cardboard tubes 15, 27–30, 32, 37
carers 11–12, 32, 45, 64
cats 20, 21–2
child-centred learning 1
Cinderella 16, 81
communication 65; bags, boxes and tubes 13; games 71;
    hair-related items 34; number lines 46; paperware 2, 5;
    play 76; puppets 16
confidence 43, 70, 71, 76
cooperation 70, 71
counting 20, 25–6, 66; biscuits 53; boxes 24; calendars 62;
    'Five Little Speckled Frogs' 52; flowers on hooks 53–5;
    game boards 78, 80–5; greeting cards 63; hair-related
    items 34; 'Nine Hairy Monsters' 49–51; number lines
    39, 46; paperware 3, 4, 5; pegs 58; penguins 62; 'Ten in the
    Bed' 28
creativity 32, 76
critical thinking 5, 66

dice 24–7, 38–9, 43–4, 58, 63, 69, 85
dinosaur landscape 28–9
direction 34, 44
disabilities 66
dominoes 6, 26
dough 7, 72, 86
drainpipe 37–9, 40

English language learners 11
envelopes 56

'Five Little Monkeys' 33
'Five Little Speckled Frogs' 19–20, 51–3, 60–1
flowers on hooks 53–5
food 27, 53
frog beanbags 51–3

games 19–20, 66–72; benefits of 77; dice 24–7, 69; game
    boards 72, 78–85; maths 32–3, 71; number lines 64;
    paperware 6–10, 11–12; pegs 57–8; resources for 69–72;
    shower caps 43–4
The Gingerbread Man 16
greeting cards 62–4
grids 82–3
group talk 11
The Gruffalo 16

hair scrunchies 35, 37, 40
hairbands 35, 40
hair-related items 34–45
hats 16, 27, 87; *see also* shower caps
hexagon game board 79–80
hiding 20
home-school relationships 71
hooks 54, 55–6
Hungry Caterpillar games 20

ice city 29
'Incy Wincy Spider' 25, 36–9
independence 77
instructions 2, 13, 71

'journey' games 81–2

kitchen rolls 10–11, 27
knitted socks 58–60
knitting wool 73–5

language 65, 66; bags, boxes and tubes 13; English language
    learners 11; hair-related items 34, 35; number lines 46;
    paperware 2, 5; play 76; puppets 16
learning 77
letters on houses 55–6
listening 13, 16, 34, 46, 65

'Mary, Mary, Quite Contrary' 53
mathematics 46, 66; bags, boxes and tubes 14;
    games 32–3, 71, 80, 85; hair-related items 35;
    paperware 3–4, 5; visual elements 11; *see also* number lines;
    numbers
measures 14, 35, 66
minibeasts 58
mobiles 30
motivation 77
movement 34